C000005828

BOURNEMOUTH

ESTATE PUBLICATIONS
Bridewell House,
Tenterden, Kent.
TN30 6EP
Tel: 01580 764225

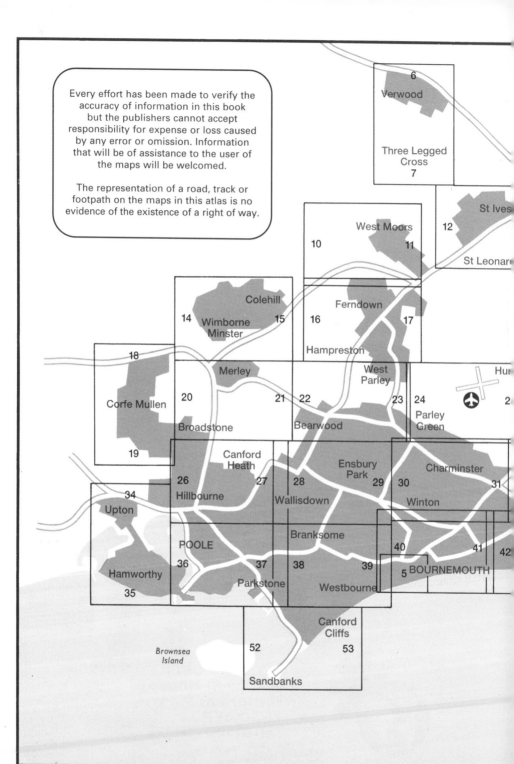

Every effort has been made to verify the accuracy of information in this book but the publishers cannot accept responsibility for expense or loss caused by any error or omission. Information that will be of assistance to the user of the maps will be welcomed.

The representation of a road, track or footpath on the maps in this atlas is no evidence of the existence of a right of way.

6 Verwood

Three Legged Cross 7

St Ives

12

St Leonar

West Moors

10   11

Colehill

14   Wimborne   15   16   Ferndown   17
     Minster

Hampreston

18

Merley   West
                Parley   Hur

Corfe Mullen   20   21   22   23   24   2

Broadstone   Bearwood   Parley
                                    Green

19

Canford   Ensbury
Heath   Park   Charminster

26   27   28   29   30   31
Hillbourne   Wallisdown   Winton

34
Upton   Branksome

                                40   41   42
POOLE   37   38   39   5 BOURNEMOUTH
36
Hamworthy   Westbourne
Parkstone
35
                Canford
                Cliffs
Brownsea   52   53
Island

Sandbanks

E S T A T E   P U B L I C A T I O N S

BOURNEMOUTH

CHRISTCHURCH   WIMBORNE MINSTER
RINGWOOD   POOLE

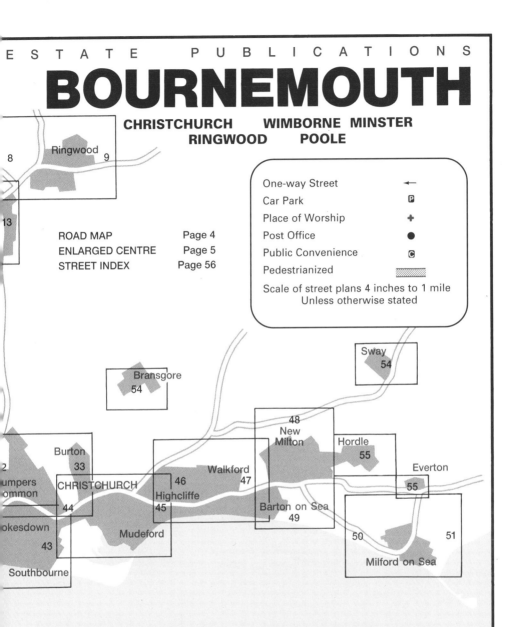

ROAD MAP	Page 4
ENLARGED CENTRE	Page 5
STREET INDEX	Page 56

One-way Street	←
Car Park	P
Place of Worship	✠
Post Office	●
Public Convenience	C
Pedestrianized	/////

Scale of street plans 4 inches to 1 mile
Unless otherwise stated

Ringwood 8 9
13
Sway 54
Bransgore 54
Burton 33
Jumpers Common
CHRISTCHURCH
Walkford 47
46
New Milton 48
Hordle 55
Everton 55
Highcliffe 45
44
Barton on Sea 49
Stokesdown 43
Mudeford
50
51
Milford on Sea
Southbourne

Street plans prepared and published by ESTATE PUBLICATIONS, Bridewell House, TENTERDEN, KENT, and based upon the ORDNANCE SURVEY mapping with the permission of The Controller of H. M. Stationery Office.

The publishers acknowledge the co-operation of the local authorities of towns represented in this atlas.

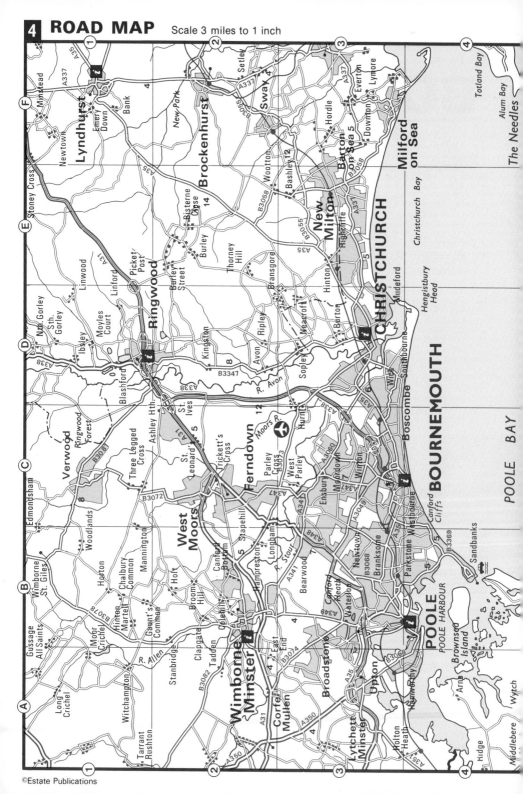

4 ROAD MAP   Scale 3 miles to 1 inch

©Estate Publications

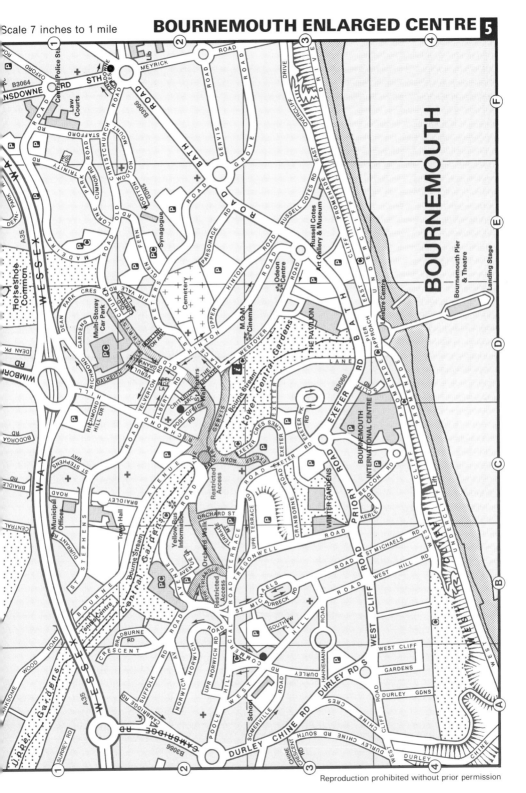

Scale 7 inches to 1 mile

BOURNEMOUTH

Bournemouth Pier & Theatre

Landing Stage

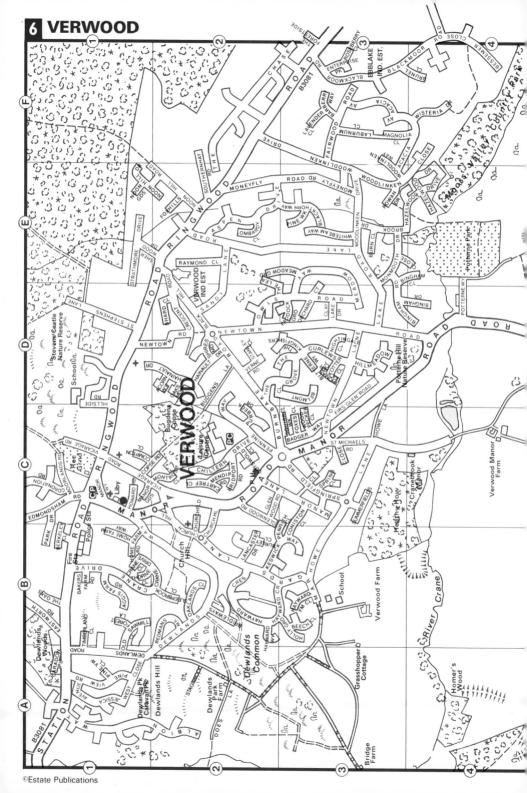

6 VERWOOD

©Estate Publications

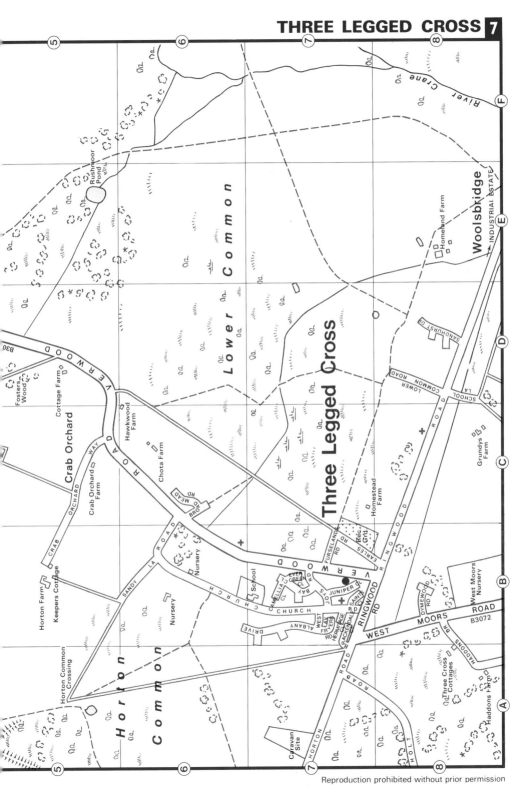

Three Legged Cross

Lower Common

Crab Orchard

Horton Common

Woolsbridge

River Crane

Labels and features:
- Rushmoor Pond
- Fosters Wood
- Cottage Farm
- Hawkwood Farm
- Chota Farm
- Crab Orchard Farm
- Horton Farm
- Keepers Cottage
- Horton Common Crossing
- Homeland Farm
- INDUSTRIAL ESTATE
- Grundys Farm
- Homestead Farm
- West Moors Nursery
- Three Cross Cottages
- Haddons Farm
- Caravan Site
- School
- Nursery
- Reg. Grd.
- VERWOOD ROAD
- B3081
- ORCHARD WAY
- CRAB
- SANDY LA
- CHURCH ROAD
- BROOM MEAD RD
- LA ROAD
- CHURCH
- WEST DRIVE
- ALBANY
- CAMELLIA CL
- EVERGREEN CL
- BAY RD
- JUNIPER
- FRYERS
- HERMITAGE
- MACKENDALE
- SANDS
- RINGWOOD RD
- FURSELANDS RD
- EARLES RD
- RINGWOOD ROAD
- LOWER COMMON ROAD
- SCHOOL LA
- SANDHURST DR
- HORTON ROAD
- HOLT ROAD
- DYMEWOOD RD
- HADDONS
- WEST MOORS ROAD
- B3072

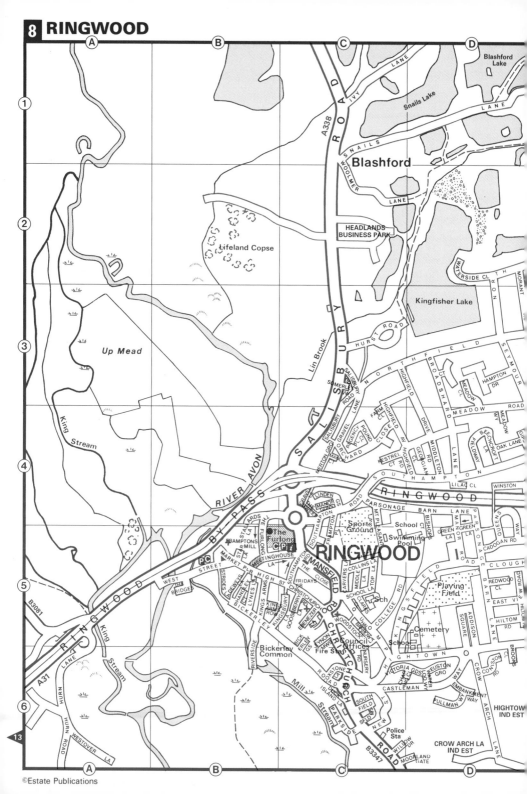

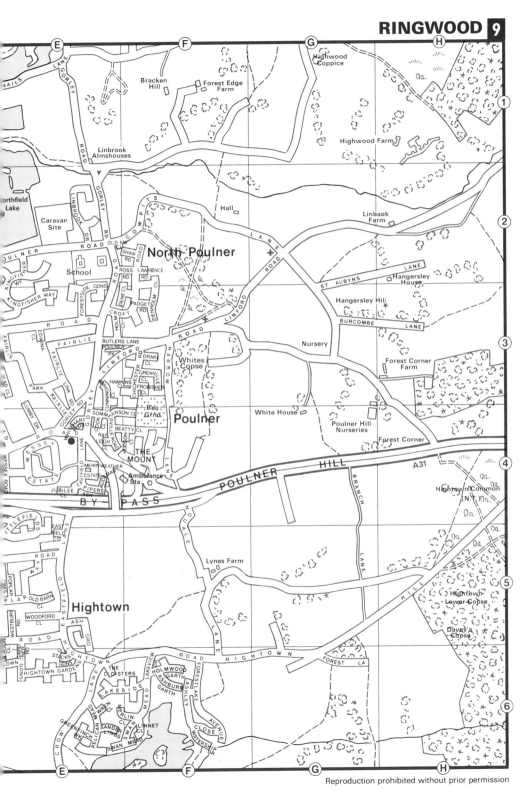

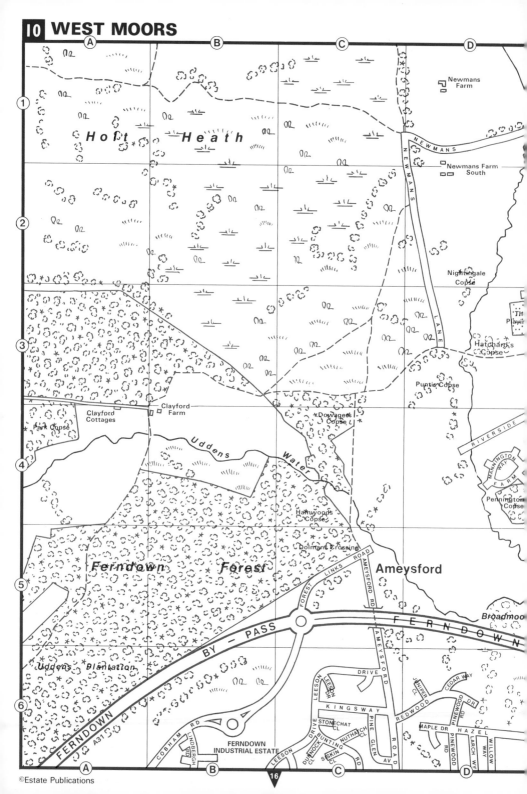

Holt Heath

Newmans Farm

Newmans Farm South

Newmans Lane

Nightingale Copse

Hatchard's Copse

Puntie Copse

Clayford Cottages

Clayford Farm

Park Copse

Uddens Water

Dowager Copse

Hannington Farm

Pennington Copse

Riverside

Hallwoods Copse

Dolmans Crossing

Ferndown Forest

Ameysford

Forest Links Road

Ameysford Rd

FERNDOWN

Broadmoor

BY-PASS

Uddens Plantation

FERNDOWN A31

Cobham Rd

Lindbergh Rd

FERNDOWN INDUSTRIAL ESTATE

Leeson Drive

Leeson Drive

Dunnock Cl

Bunting Cl

Stonechat Cl

Siskin Cl

Nuthatch Cl

Pine Glen

Ameysford Road

Kingsway

Redwood Rd

Juniper Cl

Cedar Way

Pinewood Dr

Pinewood Rd

Maple Dr

Larch Way

Hazel Way

Willow Way

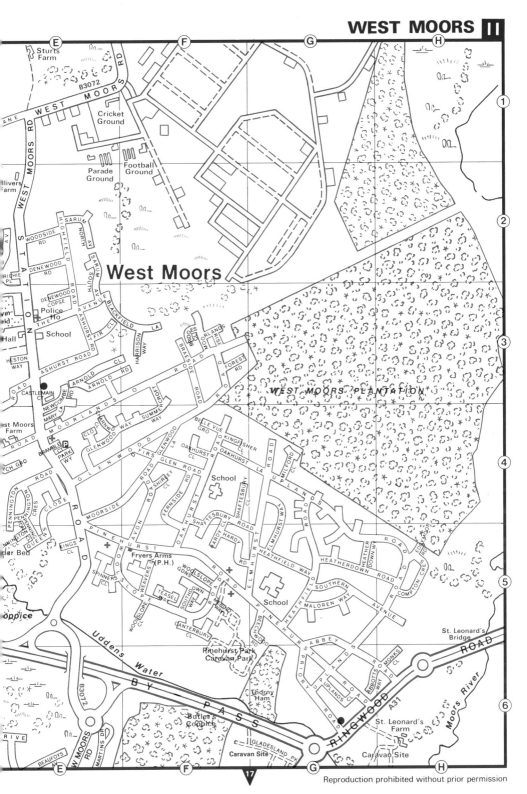

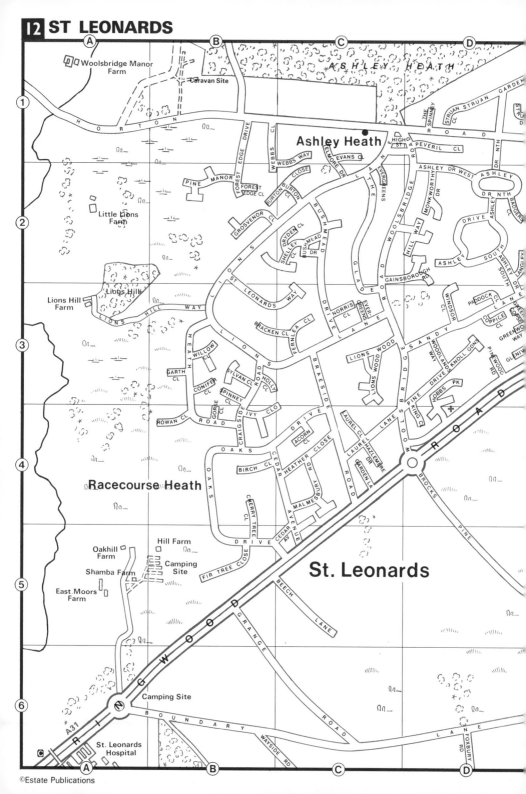

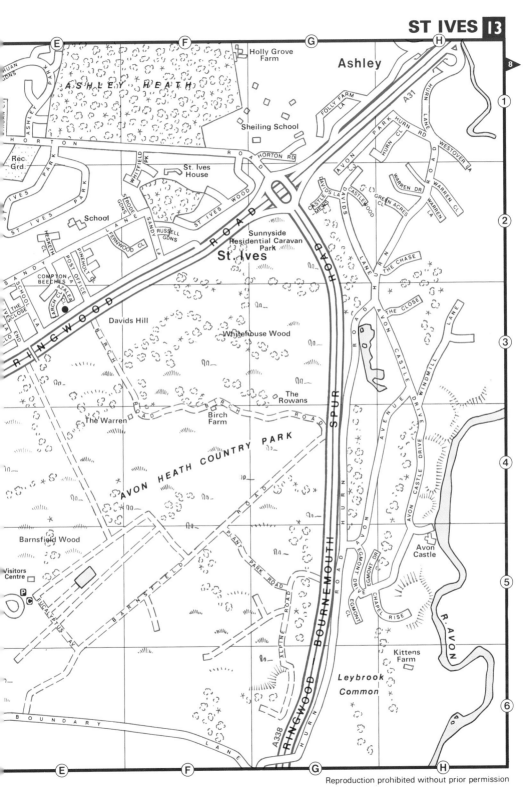

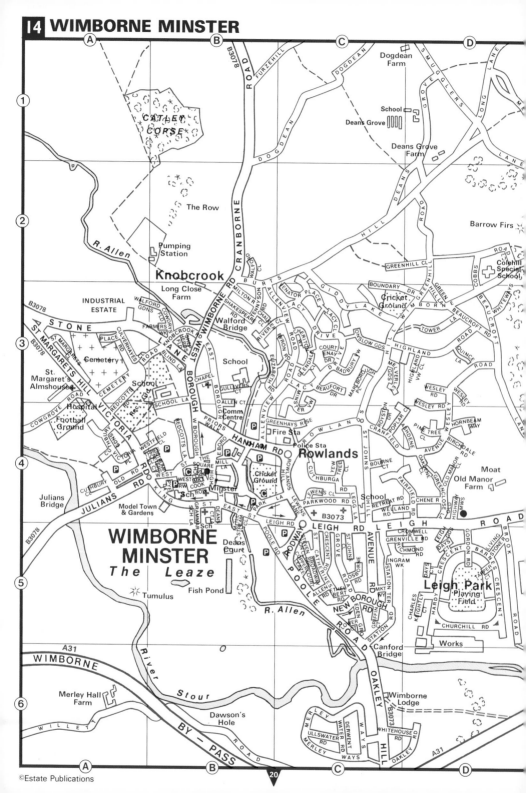

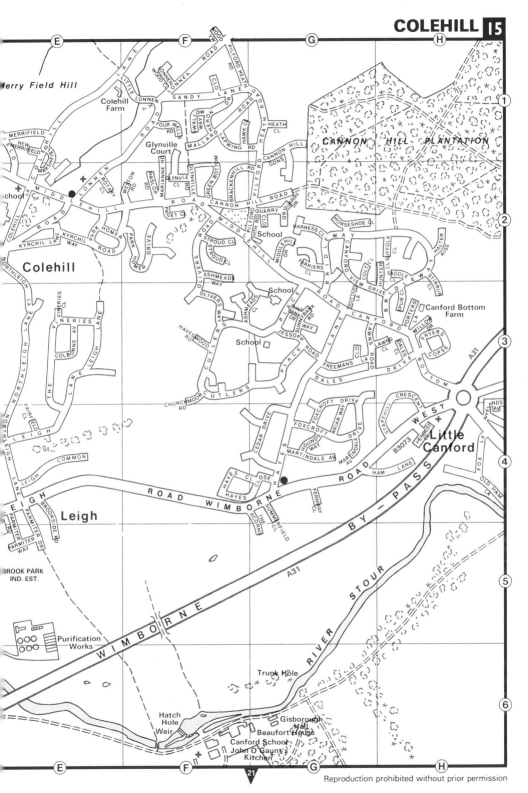

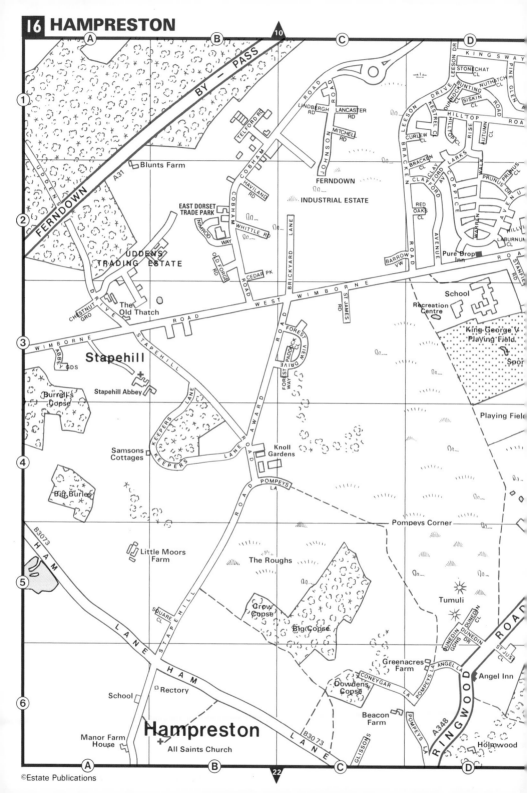

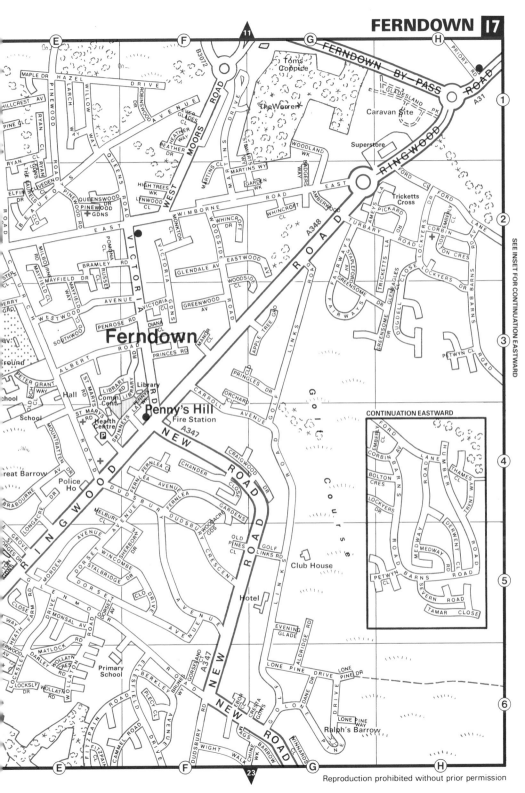

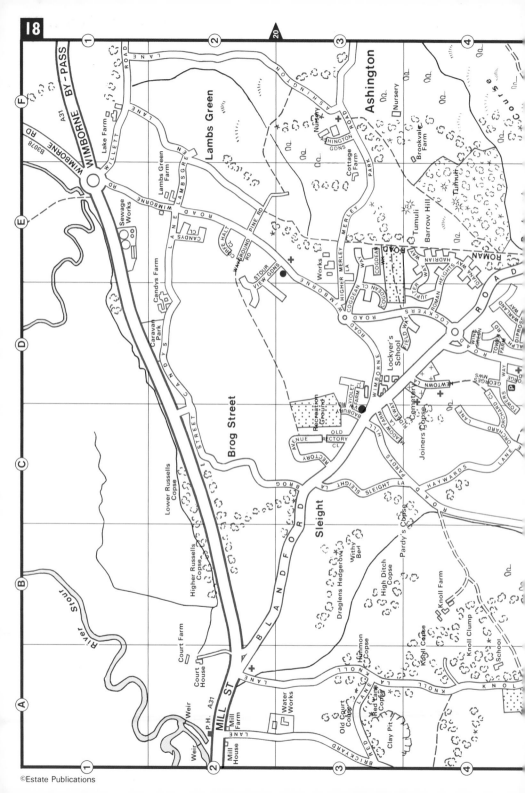

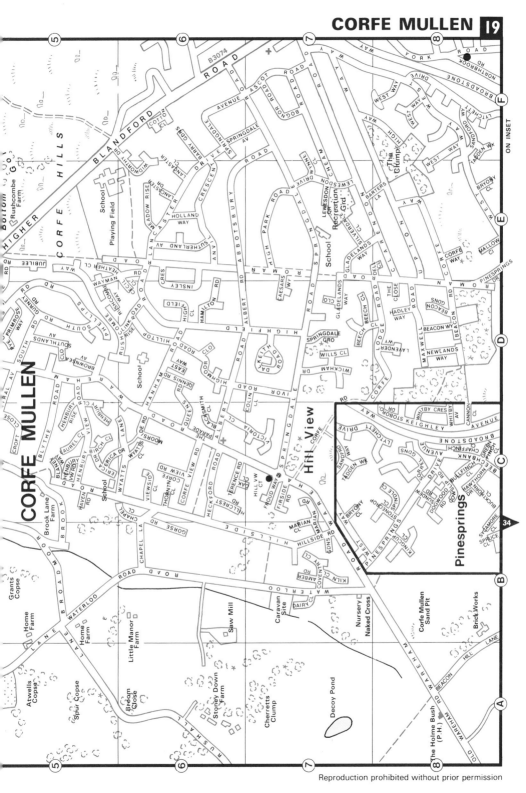

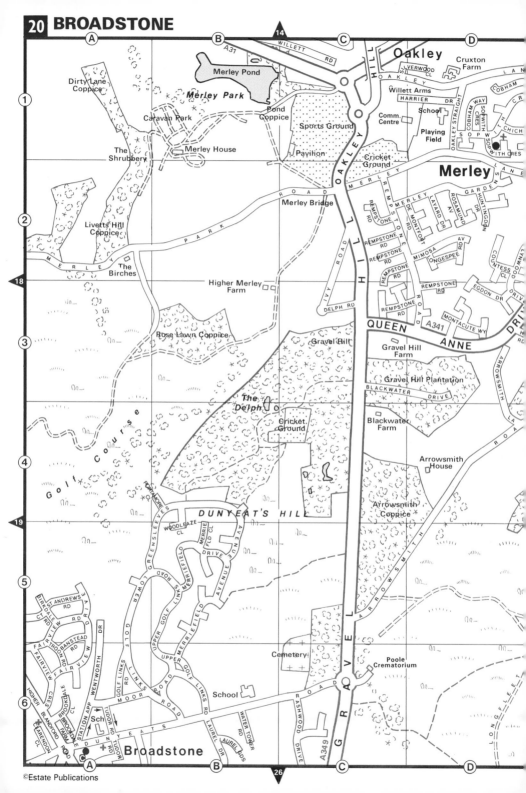

Oakley

Merley

Broadstone

©Estate Publications

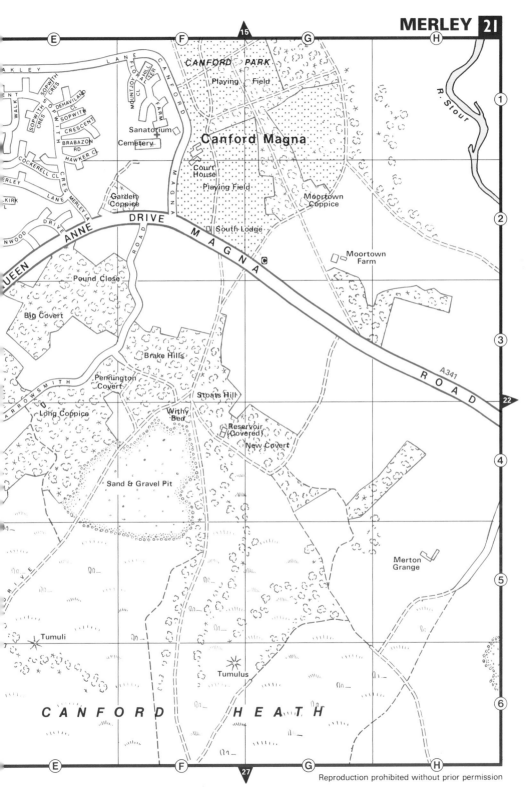

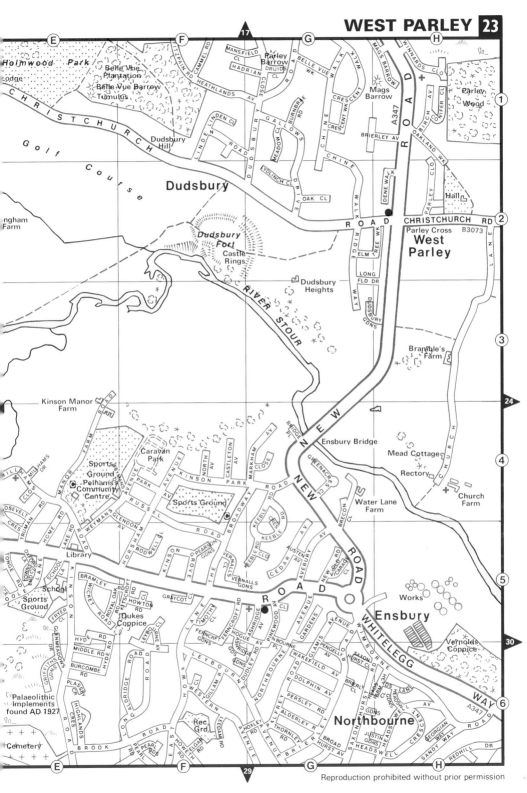

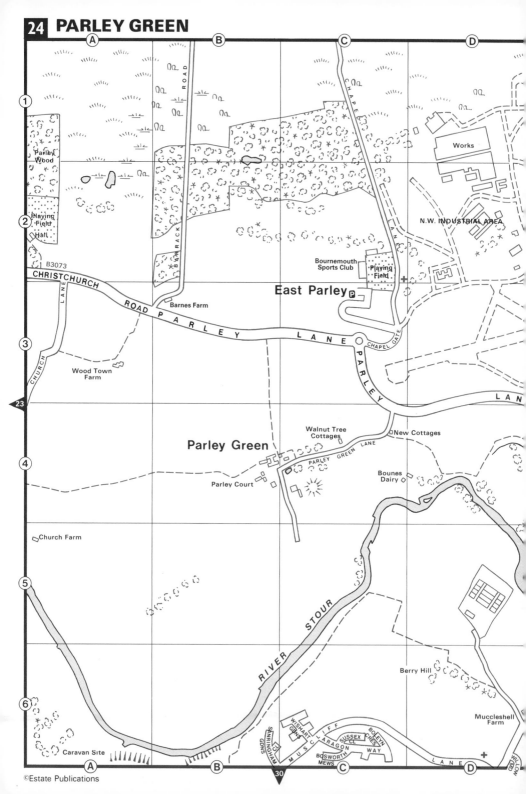

Parley Wood

Playing Field

Hall

B3073

CHRISTCHURCH

ROAD

PARLEY

LANE

Barnes Farm

East Parley

Bournemouth Sports Club

Playing Field

CHAPEL GATE

N.W. INDUSTRIAL AREA

Works

ROAD

BARRACK

LANE

CHAPEL

CHURCH LANE

Wood Town Farm

PARLEY

LANE

Parley Green

Walnut Tree Cottages

New Cottages

PARLEY GREEN LANE

Parley Court

Bounes Dairy

Church Farm

RIVER STOUR

Berry Hill

Muccleshell Farm

Caravan Site

SANDRINGHAM GDNS

WISTARIA GDNS

MUSCLIFF

ARAGON

BOSWORTH MEWS

SUSSEX WAY

BOLEYN CRES

LANE

WILLOW

23

30

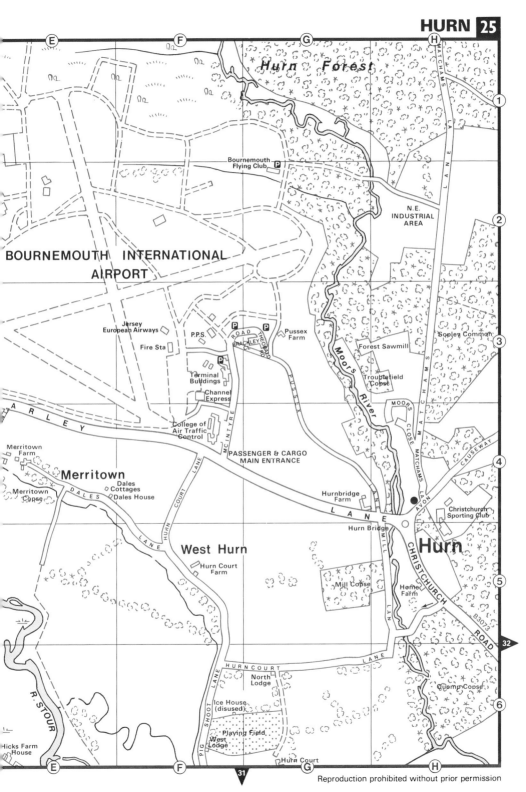

Hurn Forest

E   F   G   H

Bournemouth
Flying Club   P

N.E.
INDUSTRIAL
AREA

BOURNEMOUTH INTERNATIONAL
AIRPORT

Jersey
European Airways
P.P.S.   P   P   Pussex
Fire Sta   Farm

Sopley Common

Forest Sawmill

BRACKLEY CL   THEOBALD RD   ROAD

Terminal
Buildings   P

Channel
Express

Troublefield
Copse

College of
Air Traffic
Control

MCINTYRE

PASSENGER & CARGO
MAIN ENTRANCE

MOORS CLOSE   MATCHAMS LANE

CAUSEWAY

MOORS River   PUSSEX

Merritown
Farm

ARLEY

Merritown

Merritown
Copse

Dales
Cottages
Dales House

DALES LANE

HURN COURT LANE

LANE

Hurnbridge
Farm

Christchurch
Sporting Club

West Hurn

Hurn Bridge

HURNMILL LANE

Hurn

CHRISTCHURCH ROAD

Hurn Court
Farm

Mill Copse

Home
Farm

B3073

HURNCOURT LANE

PIG SHOOT LANE

North
Lodge

Ice House
(disused)

Playing Field

West
Lodge

Quomp Copse

R. STOUR

Hicks Farm
House

Hurn Court

E   F   G   H

1
2
3
4
5
6

32

31

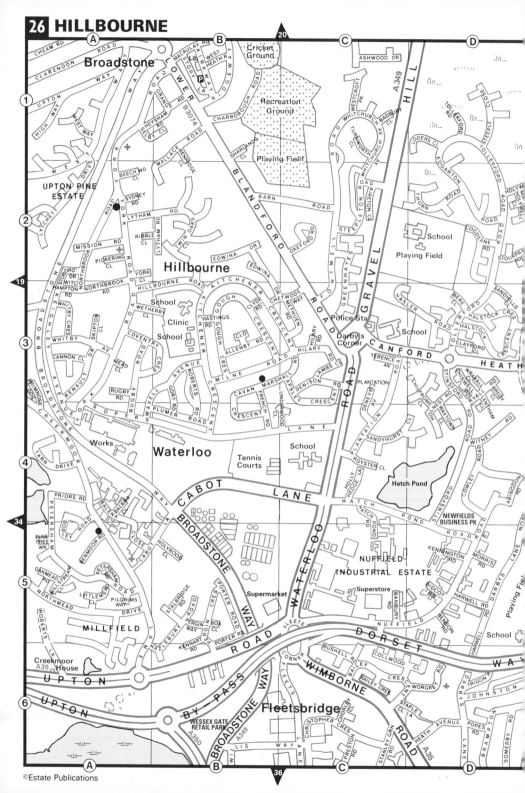

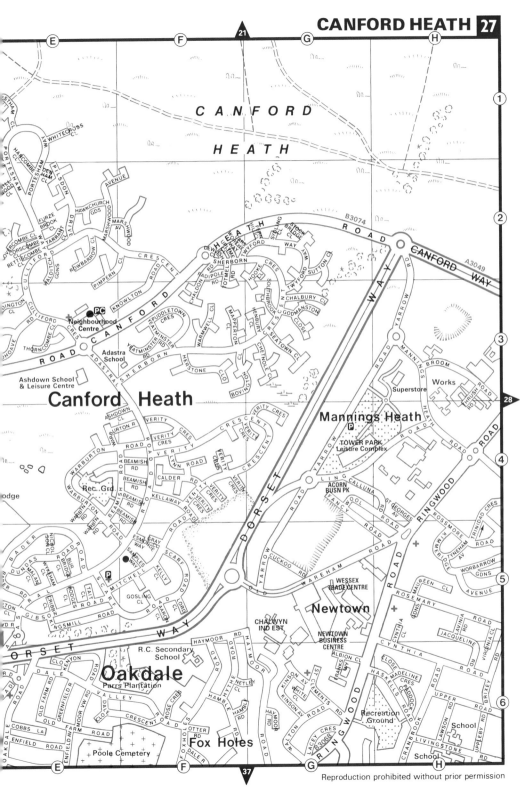

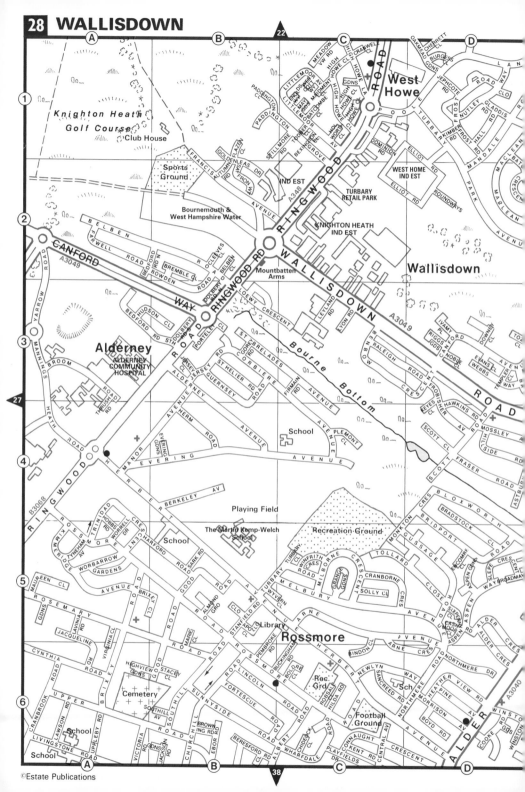

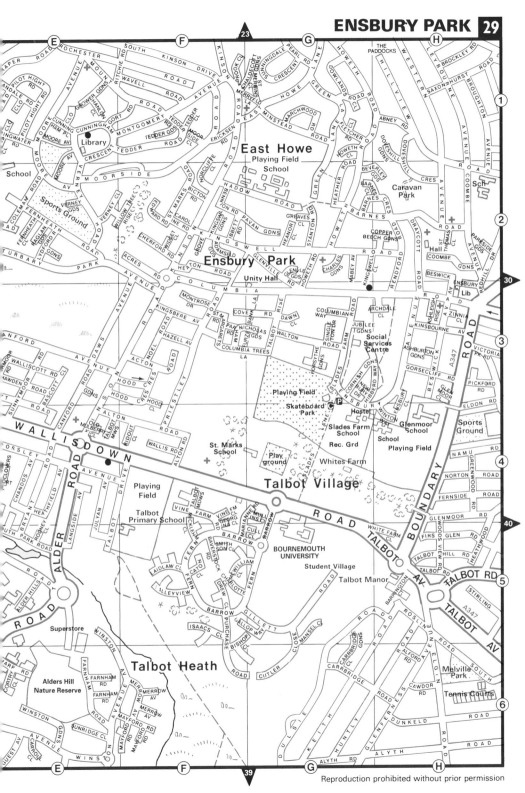

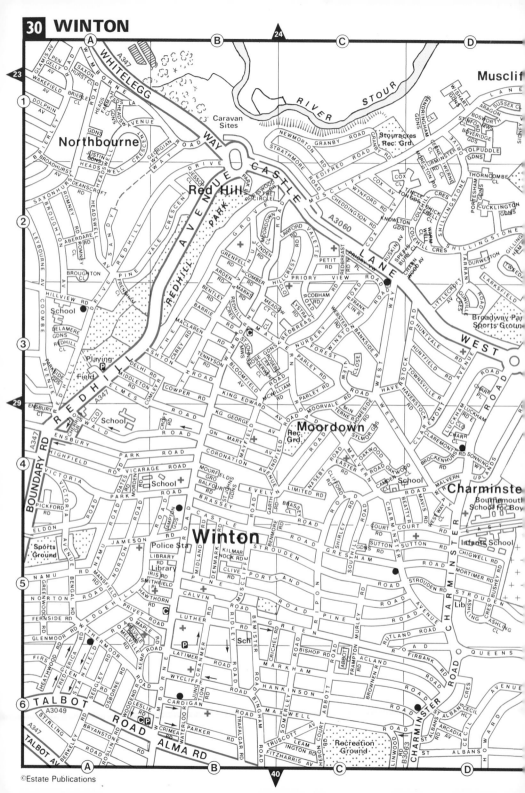

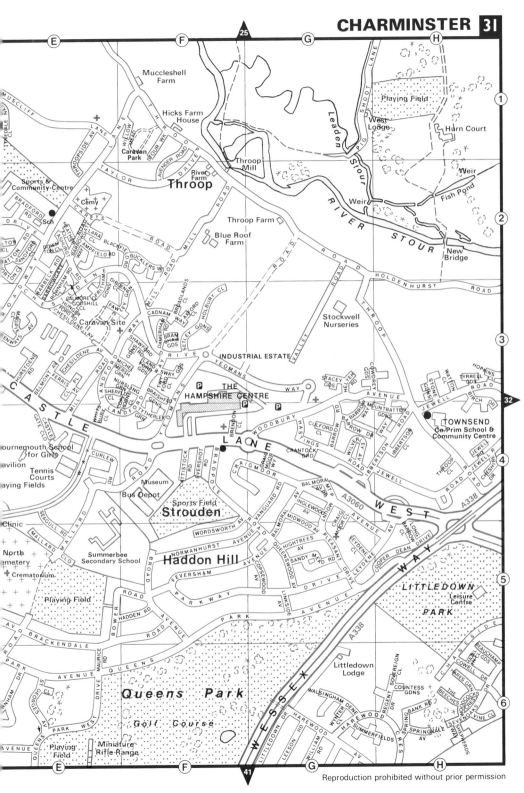

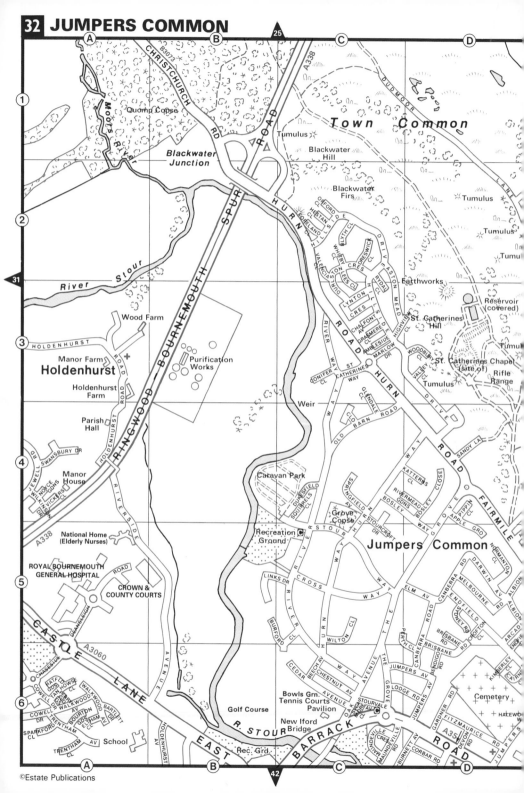

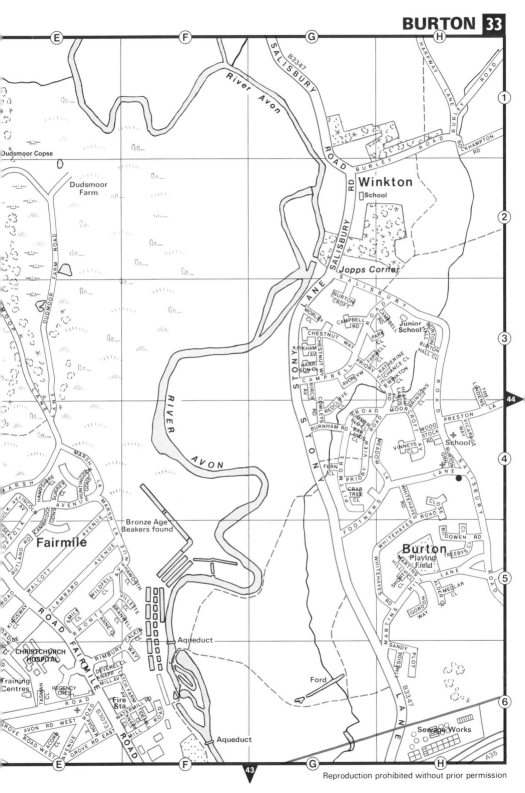

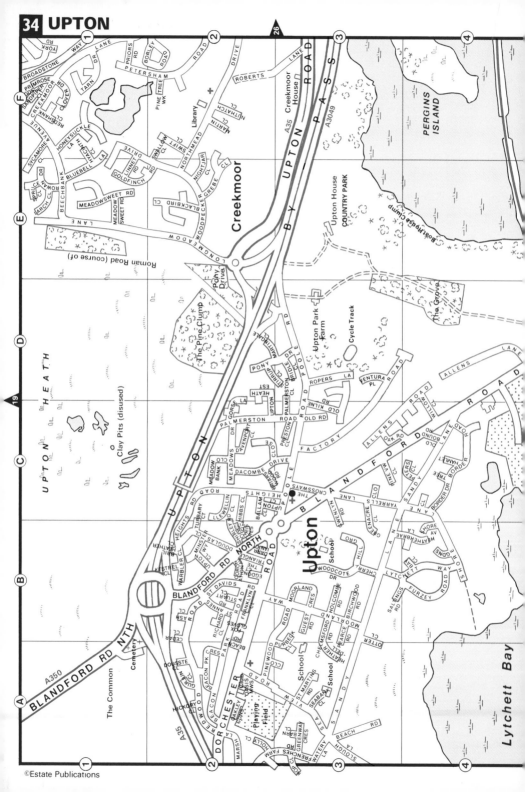

Creekmoor

Upton

PERGINS ISLAND

Lytchett Bay

UPTON HEATH

Upton House COUNTRY PARK

The Pine Clump

Clay Pits (disused)

Roman Road (course of)

Playing Field

The Common

Cemetery

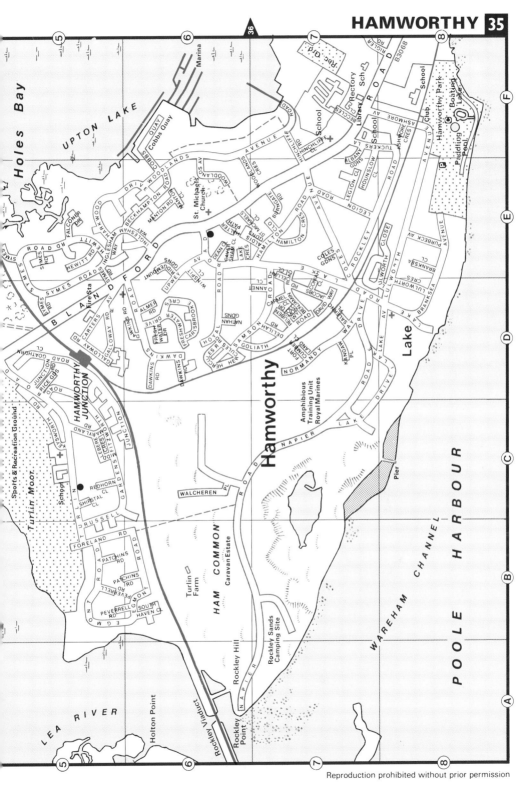

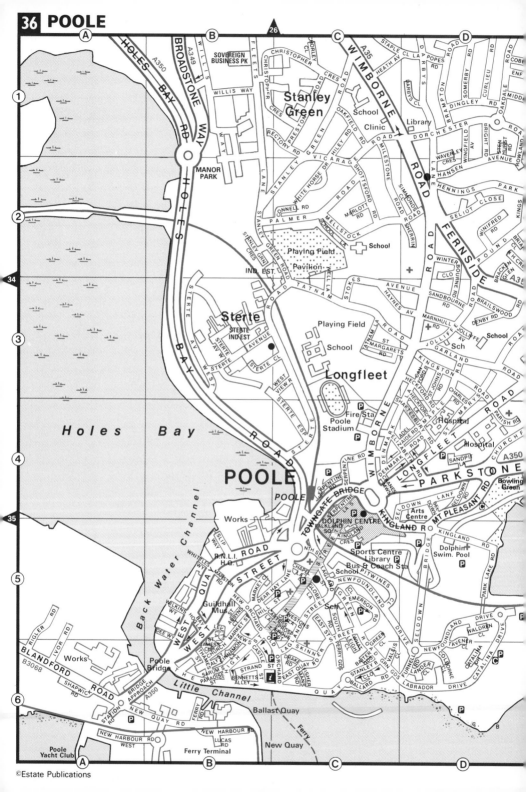

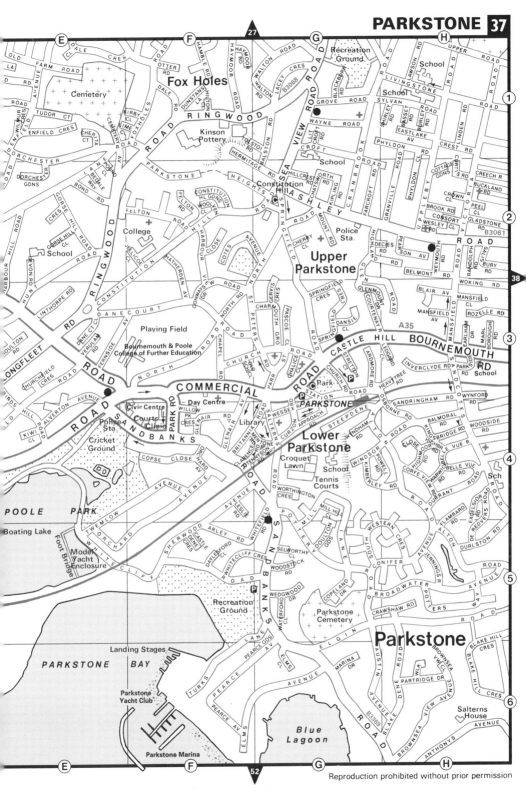

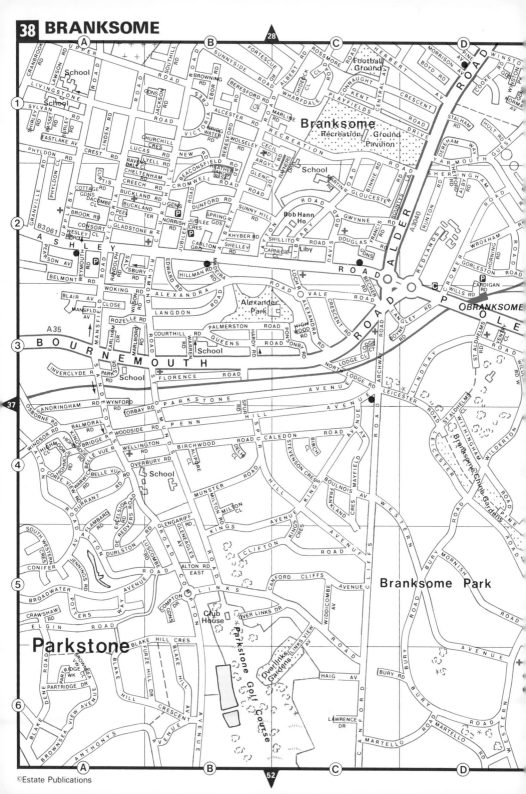

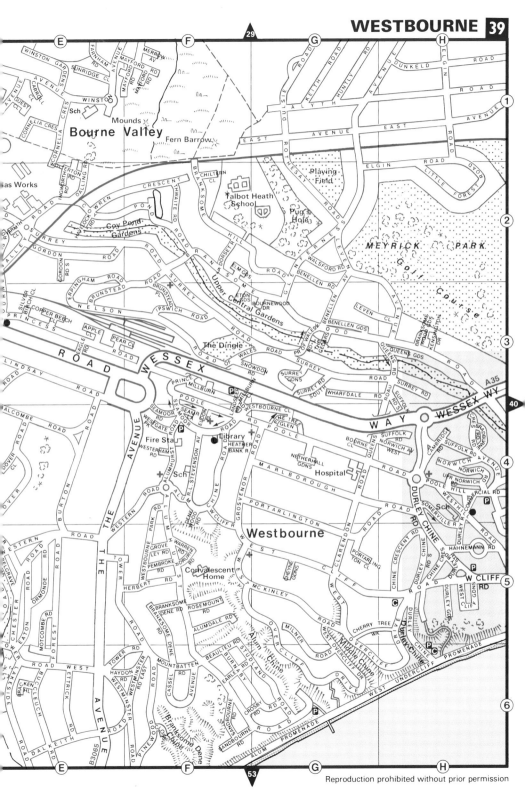

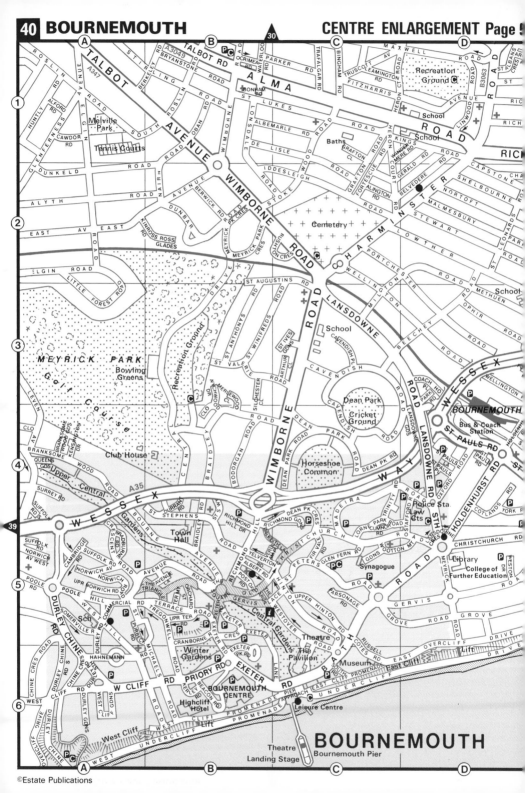

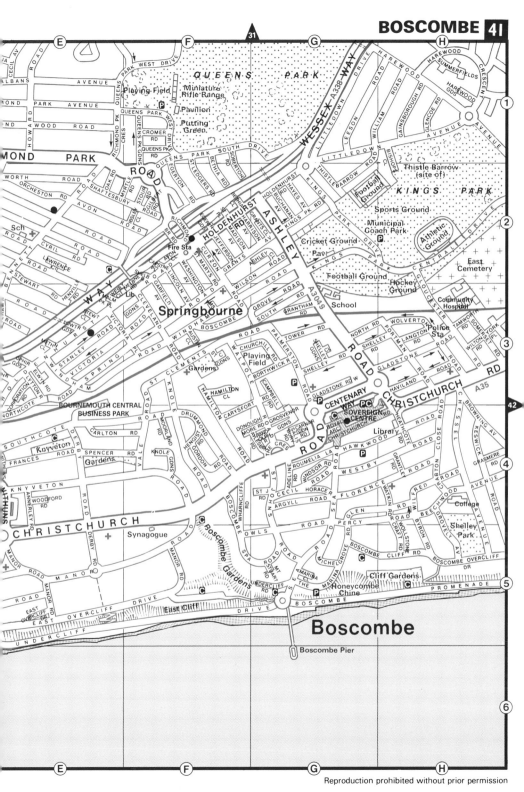

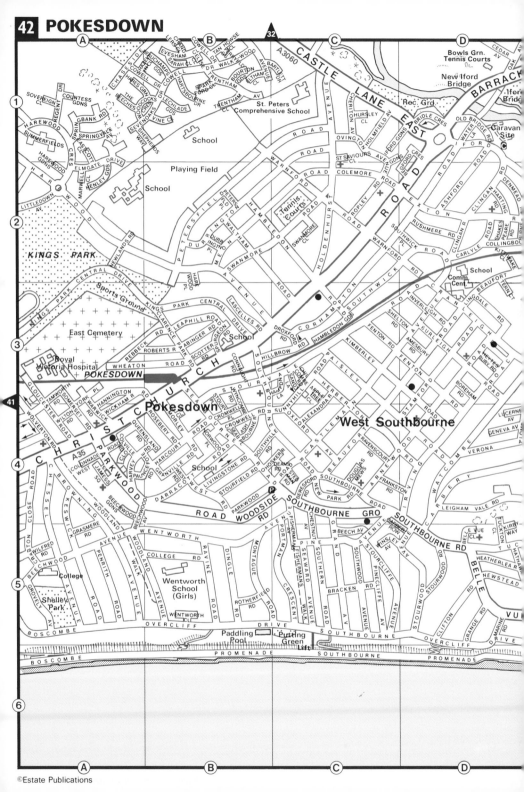

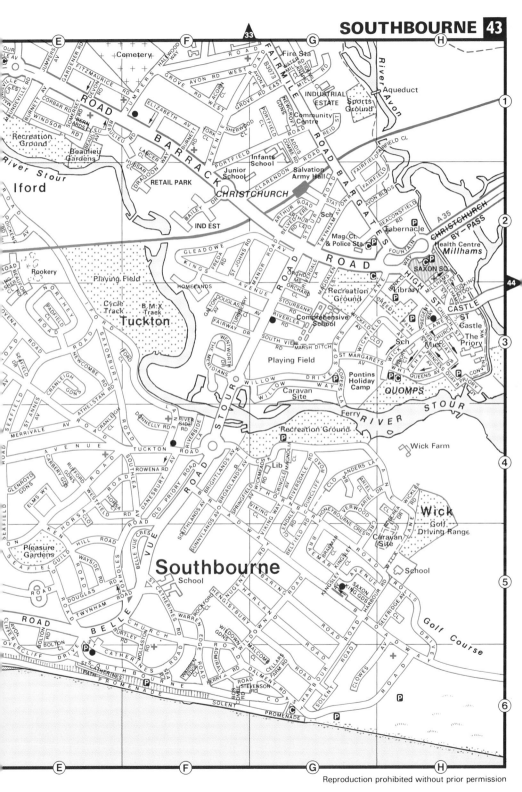

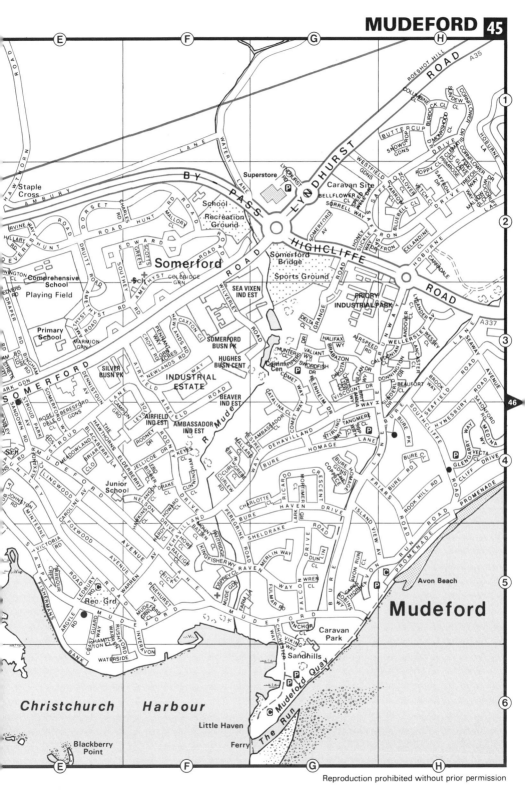

Mudeford

Somerford

Christchurch Harbour

Little Haven

Ferry

Blackberry Point

Sandhills

Caravan Park

Mudeford Quay

The Run

Avon Beach

Staple Cross

Comprehensive School
Playing Field

Primary School

Junior School

School
Recreation Ground

Superstore

Caravan Site

Somerford Bridge
Sports Ground

PRIORY INDUSTRIAL PARK

SEA VIXEN IND EST

SOMERFORD BUSN PK

SILVER BUSN PK

INDUSTRIAL ESTATE

HUGHES BUSN CENT

BEAVER IND EST

AMBASSADOR IND EST

AIRFIELD IND EST

Rec. Grd.

Waterside

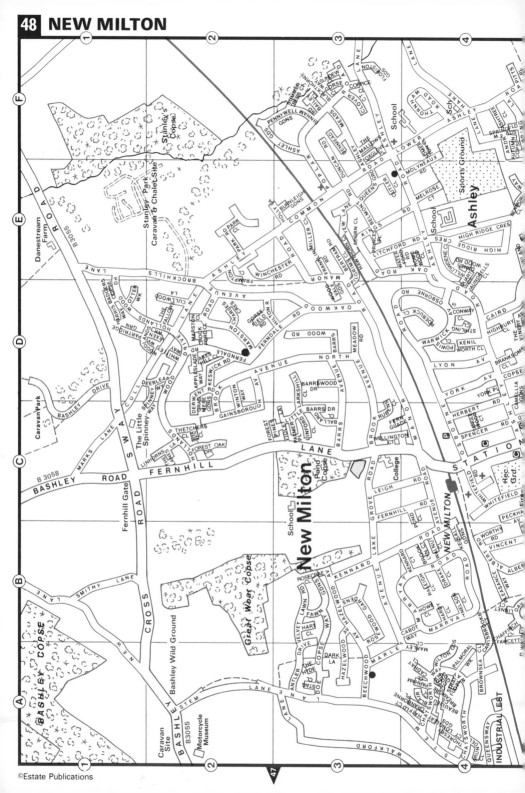

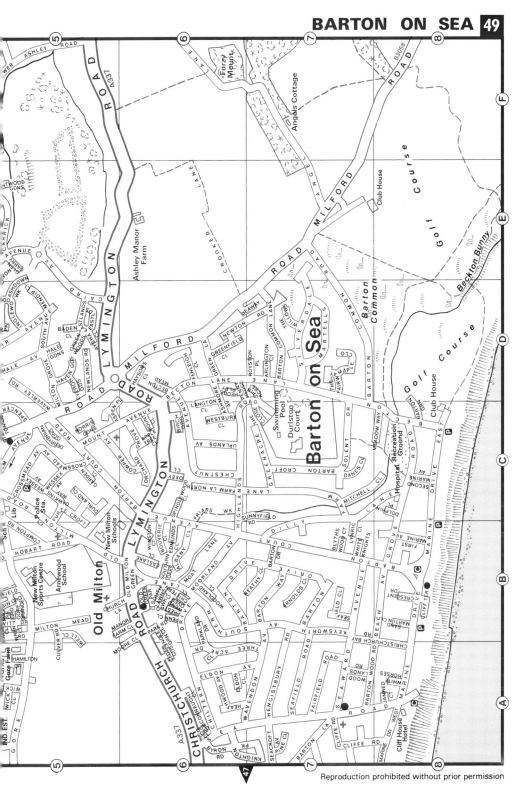

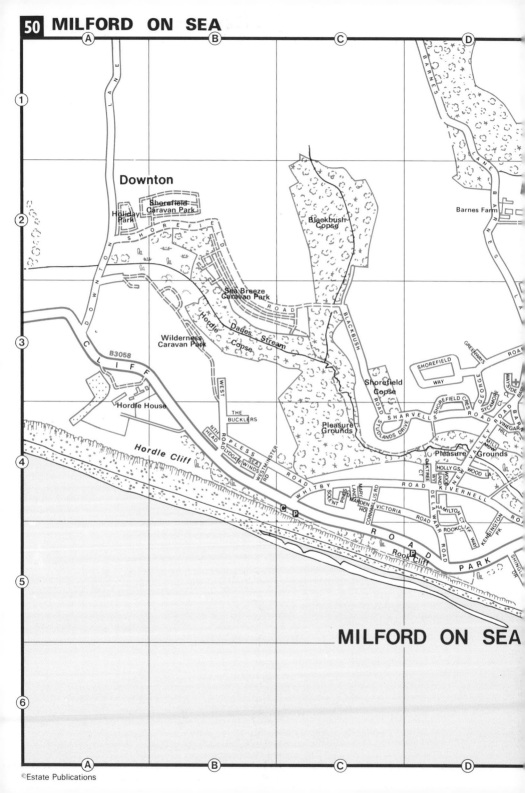

Downton

Holiday Park

Shorefield Caravan Park

Barnes Farm

Blackbush Copse

Sea Breeze Caravan Park

Wilderness Caravan Park

Hordle Copse

Danes Stream

B3058

Hordle House

WEST

THE BUCKLERS

Shorefield Copse

SHOREFIELD WAY

GREENWAYS

SHOREFIELD CRES

SHORELANDS DRIVE

SHARVELLS

GEORGE ROAD

SYCAMORE

WAYSIDE

VINEGAR HILL

Hordle Cliff

NTH HEAD

ROPLESS SEA

LYDGATE

WESTMINSTER RD

WINDS

WHITBY

Pleasure Grounds

Pleasure Grounds

OAK TREE CT

HOLLY GDS

WOOD LA

VALLEY

MILL MOW

KIVERNELL

ROAD

DE LA WARR

CLIFF WAY

HAMILTON ROAD

ROOKCLIFF

KENSINGTON PK

C P

SOLENT

MARY LANE

SPRING

MARDEN HO

CORNWALLIS RD

Victoria

ROAD

ROAD

PARK

Rook Cliff

SHINGLE

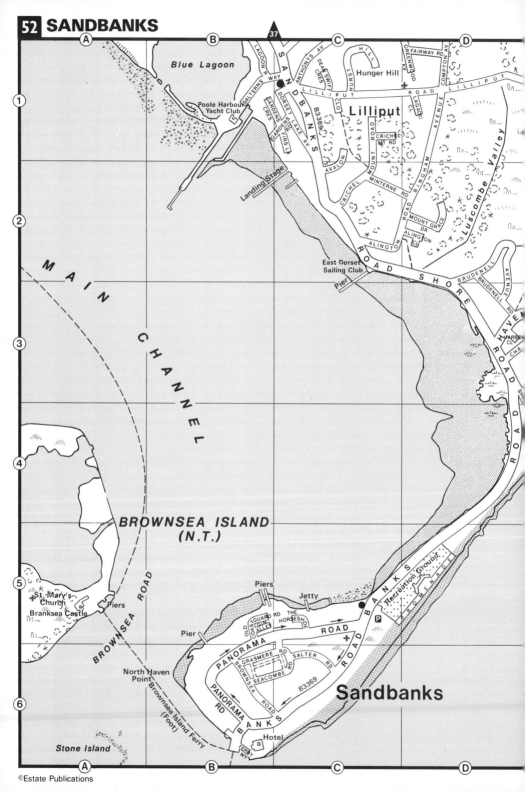

Blue Lagoon

Poole Harbour Yacht Club

SANDBANKS

LAGOON R.

HALTERNS WAY

ANTHONY'S AV

DEAN SWIFT CRES

HILL

HURST

FAIRWAY RD

GREENWOOD

COMPTON AV

LILLIPUT

Hunger Hill

Lilliput

LILLIPUT

HILL

ROAD

AVENUE

BAGRE

B3369

DORSET GARDENS CRES

DORSET GARDENS FIRS

LAKE AVS

CRICHE

MT. RD

BINGHAM

AVALON

CRICHEL

MOUNT

ROAD

MINTERNE RD

BRYCE

MOUNT GR

DR

ALINGTON CL

Luscombe Valley

Landing Stage

ALINGTON

ROAD

ALINGTON

East Dorset Sailing Club

SHORE

BRUDENELL

BRUDENELL RD

AVENUE

Pier

HAVE

HARBO CL

ROAD

CHA

SHORE

MAIN

CHANNEL

ROAD

BROWNSEA ISLAND
(N.T.)

BROWNSEA ROAD

St. Mary's Church

Branksea Castle

Piers

Piers

Jetty

THE HORSESH

Recreation Ground

BANKS

Pier

North Haven Point

OLD COASTGUARD RD

SHOP ALLEY

GRASMERE RD

SALTER RD

ROAD

P

PROMENADE

PANORAMA

BROWNSEA ROAD

SEACOMBE RD

B3369

Sandbanks

PANORAMA RD

BANKS

Brownsea Island Ferry (Foot)

Hotel

FERRY WY

Stone Island

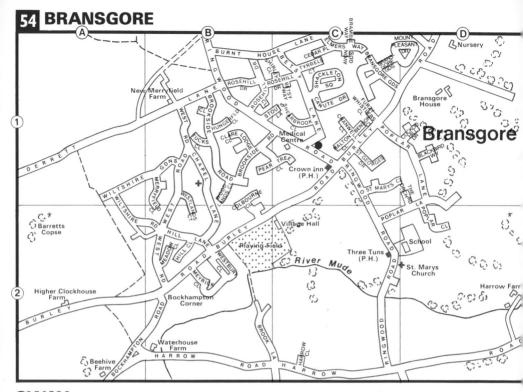

SWAY

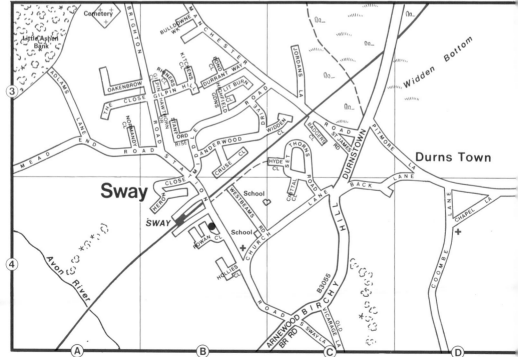

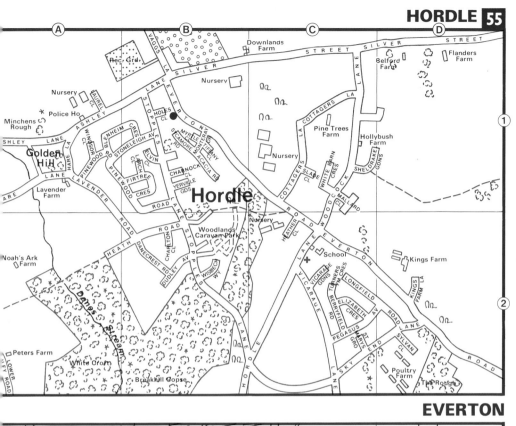

EVERTON

A - Z INDEX TO STREETS
with Postcodes

The Index includes some names for which there is insufficient space on the maps. These names are preceded by an * and are followed by the nearest adjoining thoroughfare.

Aaron Clo. BH17 27 F5
Abbey Gdns. BH22 16 A3
Abbey Rd. BH22 11 G5
Abbots Clo. BH23 46 C5
Abbotsbury Rd. BH18 19 E6
Abbott Clo. BH9 30 C6
Abbott Rd. BH9 30 C6
Abbotts Way. BH22 11 G6
Aberdare Rd. BH10 30 A2
Abingdon Dri. BH23 47 F5
Abingdon Rd. BH24 26 D4
Abinger Rd. BH7 42 B3
Abney Rd. BH10 29 H1
Acacia Av. BH31 6 F3
Acacia Rd. SO41 55 B1
Acland Rd. BH9 30 C6
Acorn Business Pk. BH12 27 G4
Acorn Clo. BH25 48 E3
Acorn Clo. BH24 12 C4
Acorn Clo. BH23 43 F1
Acorn Way. BH31 6 D2
Acres Rd. BH11 29 F2
Acton Rd. BH9 29 F3
Adamsfield Gdns. BH10 29 F2
Adastral Rd. BH17 27 E5
Addington Pl. BH23 44 D4
Addiscombe Rd. BH23 43 G1
Addison Sq. BH24 8 D5
Adelaide Clo. BH23 33 E6
Adelaide La. BH1 5 D2
Adelaide Rd. BH15 36 D4
Adeline Rd. BH5 41 G4
Adlams La. SO41 54 A3
Admiralty Rd. BH6 43 F6
Agarton La. SO41 51 F2
Aggis Farm Rd. BH31 6 B1
Airetons Clo. BH18 26 C2
Airfield Ind Est. BH23 45 F4
Airfield Rd. BH23 45 F4
Airfield Way. BH23 45 F3
Airspeed Rd. BH23 45 G3
Akeshill Clo. BH25 48 D2
Albany Clo. BH25 49 B6
Albany Dri. BH21 7 B7
Albany Gdns. BH15 35 F7
Albemarle Rd. BH3 40 B1
Albert Rd. BH1 5 C2
Albert Rd. BH12 38 B2
Albert Rd. BH21 19 C6
Albert Rd. BH22 17 E3
Albert Rd. BH25 48 B4
Albion Clo. BH15 27 G6
Albion Rd. BH23 32 D5
Albion Way. BH31 6 A2
Alby Rd. BH12 38 D2
Alcester Rd. BH12 38 B1
Alder Clo. BH23 33 H5
Alder Clo. BH25 28 D5
Alder Hills. BH12 29 E5
Alder Rd. BH12 38 C2
Alderley Rd. BH10 23 G6
Alderney Av. BH12 28 B3
Aldis Clo. BH15 35 E7
Aldridge Rd. BH22 17 G6
Aldridge Rd. BH10 23 F6
Alexander Clo. BH23 45 E4
Alexandra Rd. BH14 38 B3
Alexandra Rd. BH6 42 C4
Alford Rd. BH3 29 H6
Alington Clo. BH14 52 D2
Alington Rd. BH14 52 C2
Alington Rd. BH3 40 C2
Alipore Clo. BH14 38 B4
Allen Ct. BH21 14 B3
Allen Rd. BH21 14 C5
Allenby Clo. BH17 26 B3
Allenby Rd. BH17 26 B3
Allens La. BH16 34 D4
Allens Rd. BH16 34 C3
Allenview Rd. BH21 14 B3
Alma Rd. BH9 30 B6

Almer Rd. BH15 35 D6
Almond Gro. BH12 28 B5
Alpine Rd. BH24 13 G6
Alton Rd. BH14 37 G4
Alton Rd. BH10 29 F4
Alton Rd East. BH14 38 B5
Alum Chine Rd. BH4 39 F4
Alum Promenade. BH4 39 G6
Alumdale Rd. BH4 39 F5
Alumhurst Rd. BH4 39 F4
Alverton Av. BH15 37 E4
Alyth Rd. BH3 39 G1
Ambassador Clo. BH23 45 G4
Ambassador Ind Est. BH23 45 F4
Amber Rd. BH21 19 B7
Amberley Clo. BH23 46 C4
Amberwood. BH22 17 G2
Amberwood Clo. BH23 46 D3
Amberwood Dri. BH23 46 D3
Amberwood Gdns. BH23 46 D3
Ambleside. BH23 32 C3
Ambury La. BH23 45 E2
Amesbury Rd. BH6 42 D3
Amethyst Rd. BH23 45 E3
Ameys La. BH22 17 H2
Ameysford Rd. BH22 17 E1
Ampfield Rd. BH8 31 E2
Amsterdam Sq. BH23 44 C4
Anchor Clo. BH11 22 C5
Anchor Clo. BH23 45 G5
Anchor Rd. BH11 22 C5
Anderwood Dri. SO41 54 B3
Andover Rd. BH11 45 H3
Andrew La. BH25 48 F4
Andrews Clo. BH11 29 E1
Angel La. BH25 49 E7
Angel La. BH22 16 D6
Angeline Clo. BH23 46 C4
Anjou Clo. BH10 22 A6
Anne Clo. BH23 33 E5
Annerley Rd. BH1 41 E4
Annet Clo. BH15 35 D7
Anson Clo. BH23 45 F4
Anson Clo. BH24 9 E4
Anstey Clo. BH11 22 D5
Anstey Rd. BH11 22 C6
Anthonys Av. BH14 37 H6
Antler Dri. BH25 48 A3
Anvil Clo. BH18 19 E6
Apollo Clo. BH12 28 B5
Apple Clo. BH4 39 E3
Apple Gro. BH23 32 D4
Apple Tree Clo. BH25 49 C6
Apple Tree Gro. BH22 17 G3
Appletree Clo. BH8 42 C3
Approach Rd. BH14 37 G4
Apsley Cres. BH17 26 C3
Aragon Way. BH9 30 D1
Arcadia Av. BH8 30 D6
Arcadia Rd. BH23 32 D5
Archdale Clo. BH10 29 H3
Archway Rd. BH14 38 C3
Arden Rd. BH9 30 B2
Arden Walk. BH25 48 D4
Ardmore Rd. BH14 37 G3
Argyle Rd. BH23 45 E5
Argyll Rd. BH5 41 G4
Argyll Rd. BH12 38 B1
Ariel Clo. BH6 43 G4
Ariel Dri. BH6 43 G4
Arley Rd. BH14 37 F5
Arlington Ct. BH25 49 D7
Arne Av. BH12 28 C5
Arne Cres. BH12 28 C5
Arnewood Bridge Rd. SO41 54 C4
Arnewood Rd. BH6 42 C4
Arnold Rd. BH22 11 E3
Arnold Rd. BH22 11 E3
Arnolds Clo. BH25 49 B7
Arran Way. BH23 47 E4
Arrowsmith La. BH21 20 C5
Arrowsmith Rd. BH21 20 D3
Arthur Clo. BH7 40 C3
Arthur La. BH23 43 G2
Arthur Rd. BH23 43 G2
Arundel Clo. BH25 47 H2

Arundel Way. BH23 46 C6
Ascham Rd. BH8 41 E3
Ascot Rd. BH18 19 F7
Ash Clo. BH16 34 B2
Ash Gro. SO41 55 B4
Ash Gro. BH24 9 E5
Ashbourne Rd. BH5 42 B4
Ashburn Garth. BH24 9 F6
Ashburton Gdns. BH10 29 H3
Ashdene. BH21 14 D4
Ashdown Clo. BH17 27 E4
Ashdown Walk. BH25 49 D5
Ashford Rd. BH6 42 D2
Ashington Gdns. BH21 18 F3
Ashington La. BH21 18 F1
Ashleigh Rise. BH10 29 H3
Ashlet Gdns. BH25 48 F3
Ashley Clo. BH1 41 G2
Ashley Common Rd. BH25 9 F6
Ashley Dri. BH24 12 D2
Ashley Dri North. BH24 12 D2
Ashley Dri South. BH24 12 D2
Ashley Dri West. BH24 12 D2
Ashley La. BH25 48 F3
Ashley Meads. BH25 48 F3
Ashley Pk. BH24 13 E1
Ashley Rd. BH1 41 G2
Ashley Rd. BH25 48 C4
Ashley Rd. BH14 37 G2
Ashling Clo. BH8 30 D5
Ashling Cres. BH8 30 D5
Ashmeads Clo. BH21 15 G3
Ashmeads Way. BH21 15 F2
Ashmore Av. BH25 49 C6
Ashmore Av. BH15 35 F8
Ashmore Cres. BH15 35 F8
Ashmore Gro. BH23 46 B3
Ashridge Av. BH10 23 G5
Ashridge Gdns. BH10 23 G5
Ashton Rd. BH9 30 A3
Ashtree Clo. BH25 48 F4
Ashurst Rd. BH8 31 E2
Ashurst Rd. BH22 11 E3
Ashwood Dri. BH18 20 C6
Aspen Clo. BH31 6 E2
Aspen Gdns. BH12 28 D5
Aspen Pl. BH25 49 C5
Aspen Rd. BH12 28 D5
Aspen Way. BH12 28 D5
Asquith Clo. BH23 44 D4
Astbury Av. BH12 28 D4
Aston Mead. BH23 32 C2
Athelstan Rd. BH6 43 E4
Aubrey Clo. SO41 51 G4
Auckland Rd. BH23 46 A5
Audemar Ct. BH24 9 E4
Austen Av. BH10 23 G5
Auster Clo. BH23 45 G3
Austin Av. BH14 37 G6
Austin Clo. BH1 41 F3
Autumn Clo. BH25 16 D1
Autumn Copse. BH25 48 F4
Autumn Rd. BH11 28 B2
Avalon. BH14 52 C2
Avebury Av. BH10 23 G5
Avenue La. BH2 5 B2
Avenue Rd. BH2 5 B2
Avenue Rd, Burton. BH23 33 E6
Avenue Rd, New Milton. BH25 48 C4
Avenue Rd, Walkford. BH23 47 F3
Avenue Rd. BH11 14 C5
Avon Av. BH24 13 G5
Avon Buildings. BH23 44 C4
Avon Castle Dri. BH24 13 H3
Avon Causeway. BH23 25 H4
Avon Clo. BH8 41 F2
Avon Gdns. BH23 54 C1
Avon Pk. BH24 13 G2
Avon Rd. BH8 41 E2
Avon Rd. BH22 11 F5
Avon Rd East. BH23 33 E6
Avon Rd West. BH23 33 E6
Avon Run Clo. BH23 45 G3
Avon Run Rd. BH23 45 G3
Avon View. BH23 33 G3

Avon Wharf. BH23 44 C4
Avoncliffe Rd. BH6 43 E5
Award Rd. BH21 16 B4
Axford Clo. BH8 31 F3
Aylesbury Rd. BH1 41 G4
Aysha Clo. BH25 49 D5
Azalea Clo. BH24 13 E3

Back La. SO41 54 C4
Badbury Clo. BH18 26 C1
Badbury Vw. BH21 14 C3
Badbury Vw Rd. BH21 18 C3
Baden Clo. BH25 49 D5
Bader Rd. BH17 27 E5
Badger Way. BH31 6 C3
Badgers Clo. BH24 12 D2
Badgers Clo. SO41 54 C3
Badgers Copse. BH25 48 D1
Badgers Way. BH22 17 G2
Bailey Clo. BH25 48 F3
Bailey Cres. BH15 26 C6
Bailey Dri. BH23 43 F2
Baiter Gdns. BH15 36 C6
Baker Rd. BH11 22 C5
Bakers Farm Rd. BH31 6 B1
Balcombe Rd. BH13 39 E4
Baldwin Clo. BH23 44 D4
Balena Clo. BH17 26 A4
Balfour Clo. BH23 46 A4
Balfour Rd. BH9 30 B4
Ballam Clo. BH16 34 C2
Ballard Clo. BH25 48 C3
Ballard Clo. BH15 36 C6
Ballard Rd. BH15 36 C6
Balmoral Av. BH8 31 G5
Balmoral Rd. BH14 37 H4
Balmoral Walk. BH25 49 E7
Balston Rd. BH14 37 G2
Banbury Rd. BH17 26 C5
Bank Clo. BH23 43 H2
Banks Rd. BH13 52 B6
Bankside Rd. BH9 30 C3
Banstead Rd. BH18 20 A6
Barberry Way. BH31 6 F3
Barbers Gate, Thames St. BH15 36 B6
Barbers Wharf, The Quay. BH15 36 B6
Bargates. BH23 44 B3
Baring Rd. BH6 43 G5
Barlands Clo. BH23 33 G4
Barn Clo. BH16 34 A3
Barn Rd. BH18 26 B2
Barnes Clo. BH10 29 H2
Barnes Cres. BH21 14 D5
Barnes La. SO41 50 D1
Barnes Rd. BH22 17 G3
Barnfield. BH23 46 A5
Barnsfield Rd. BH24 13 E5
Barons Rd. BH11 22 A5
Barrack Rd. BH22 24 B2
Barrack Rd. BH23 42 D1
Barrie Rd. BH9 30 B3
Barrington Ct. BH3 29 H5
Barrow Dri. BH8 31 G4
Barrow Rd. BH8 31 G4
Barrow View. BH22 16 C2
Barrow Way. BH8 31 G4
Barrowgate Rd. BH8 31 E3
Barrowgate Way. BH8 31 E2
Barrs Av. BH25 48 C3
Barrs Wood Dri. BH25 48 D3
Barrs Wood Rd. BH25 48 D3
Barry Gdns. BH18 19 F6
Barters La. BH18 19 E7
Bartlett Dri. BH7 32 A6
Barton Common La. BH25 49 D7
Barton Common Rd. BH25 49 D7
Barton Court Av. BH25 49 B8
Barton Court Rd. BH25 49 C6
Barton Croft. BH25 49 C7
Barton Dri. BH25 49 B7
Barton Grn. BH25 49 C8
Barton La. BH25 49 A7
Barton Way. BH25 49 B7
Barton Wood Rd. BH25 49 A7

Bartonside Rd. BH25 47 F5
Bascott Clo. BH11 29 E3
Bascott Rd. BH11 28 D3
Bashley Cross Rd. BH25 48 A2
Bashley Dri. BH25 48 D1
Bashley Rd. BH25 48 C1
Bassett Rd. BH12 37 H1
Batchelor Cres. BH11 28 D2
Batchelor Rd. BH11 28 D1
Batcombe Clo. BH11 28 C1
Bath Rd. BH1 5 D3
Batten Clo. BH23 44 D3
Baverstock Rd. BH12 29 F5
Bay Clo. BH21 7 B7
Bay Clo. BH16 34 B4
Bay Hog La. BH15 36 B5
Bay Tree Way. BH23 46 B3
Beach Av. BH25 49 B8
Beach Rd. BH13 53 G1
Beach Rd. BH16 34 A3
Beacon Clo. SO41 55 B3
Beacon Dri. BH23 46 C5
Beacon Gdns. BH18 19 E8
Beacon Hill La. BH21 19 A8
Beacon Pk Cres. BH16 34 A2
Beacon Pk Rd. BH16 34 A2
Beacon Rd. BH2 5 C3
Beacon Rd. BH18 19 D8
Beacon Way. BH18 19 D8
Beaconsfield Rd. BH12 38 B2
Beaconsfield Rd. BH23 44 B3
Beamish Rd. BH17 27 E4
Bear Cross. BH11 22 C5
Bear Cross Av. BH11 22 B4
Beatty Clo. BH24 9 E4
Beatty Rd. BH9 30 C4
Beauchamp Gdns. BH7 31 H6
Beaucroft La. BH21 14 D3
Beaucroft Rd. BH21 14 D3
Beaufort Gdns. BH23 45 H3
Beaufort Dri. BH21 14 C3
Beaufort Rd. BH6 42 C4
Beaufoys Av. BH22 17 E2
Beaufoys Clo. BH22 17 E2
Beaulieu Av. BH23 43 E1
Beaulieu Clo. BH25 47 H2
Beaulieu Rd. BH23 43 E1
Beaulieu Rd. BH4 39 F6
Beaver Ind Est. BH23 45 F3
Beccles Clo. BH13 35 F7
Becher Rd. BH14 38 C3
Beckhampton Rd. BH15 35 E6
Beckley Copse. BH23 47 E3
Becton La. BH25 49 D6
Becton Mead. BH25 49 D6
Bedale Way. BH15 37 E2
Bedford Cres. BH7 42 D1
Bedford Rd Nth. BH12 28 A2
Bedford Rd Sth. BH12 28 A3
Beech Av. BH23 32 C6
Beech Av. BH6 42 C5
Beech Clo. BH18 19 D7
Beech Clo. SO41 55 B4
Beech Clo. BH31 6 B3
Beech La. BH24 12 C5
Beech Wood Clo. BH18 26 A2
Beechbank Av. BH18 Inset 19
Beechcroft La. BH24 8 D4
Beechey Rd. BH8 40 C3
Beechwood Av. BH5 42 A5
Beechwood Av. BH23 48 A3
Beechwood Gdns. BH5 42 A4
Beechwood Rd. BH22 11 G5
Belben Clo. BH12 28 B2
Belben Rd. BH12 28 A2
Belfield Rd. BH6 42 D5
Belgrave Rd. BH13 39 E5
Bell Heather Clo. BH6 34 B2
Belle Vue Cres. BH6 42 D5
Belle Vue Gro. BH22 11 F4
Belle Vue Rd. BH6 42 D5
Belle Vue Rd. BH14 37 H4
Belle Vue Walk. BH22 23 G1
Bellflower Clo. BH23 46 B3
Belmont Av. BH8 31 E3
Belmont Clo. BH31 6 D3
Belmont Rd. BH25 48 E3

Belmont Rd. BH14 37 H2
Belvedere Rd. BH3 40 D2
Belvedere Rd. BH23 43 G2
Bemister Rd. BH9 30 B5
Benbow Cres. BH12 28 C3
Benbridge Av. BH11 22 C5
Bendigo Rd. BH23 32 D6
Benellen Av. BH4 39 G3
Benellen Gdns. BH4 39 G3
Benellen Rd. BH4 39 G2
Bengal Rd. BH9 30 A5
Benjamin Rd. BH15 35 D7
Benmoor Rd. BH17 26 A5
Benmore Clo. BH15 48 E4
Benmore Rd. BH9 30 B5
Bennett Rd. BH8 41 E2
Bennetts Alley. BH15 36 B6
Bennion Rd. BH10 29 F2
Benridge Clo. BH18 26 B1
Benson Clo. BH23 54 C1
Benson Rd. BH17 26 D5
Bentley Rd. BH9 30 B3
Bere Clo. BH17 26 D3
Beresford Rd. BH12 38 B1
Beresford Gdns. BH23 45 E4
Beresford Rd. BH12 38 B1
Beresford Rd. BH6 42 C4
Berkeley Av. BH12 28 B4
Berkeley Clo. BH31 6 B1
Berkeley Rd. BH3 30 A6
Berkley Av. BH22 17 F6
Bernards Rd. BH23 43 E1
Berrans Av. BH11 22 D5
Berryfield Rd. SO41 55 C2
Bertram Rd. BH22 48 E3
Berwick Rd. BH3 40 B2
Bessborough Rd. BH13 53 E2
Bessemer Clo. BH11 6 F4
Beswick Av. BH10 29 H3
Bethia Clo. BH8 41 F2
Bethia Rd. BH8 41 F1
Betsy Clo. BH23 54 C1
Betsy La. BH23 54 C1
Bettiscombe Clo. BH17 27 E2
Beverley Gdns. BH10 29 G2
Bexington Clo. BH11 28 C1
Bickerley Gdns. BH24 8 C5
Bickerley Rd. BH24 8 B5
Bicton Rd. BH11 29 F2
Bindon Clo. BH12 28 C5
Bingham Av. BH14 52 D2
Bingham Rd. BH23 45 E3
Bingham Clo. BH31 6 E3
Bingham Dri. BH31 6 D4
Bingham Rd. BH23 44 D3
Bingham Rd. BH31 6 E3
Bingham Rd. BH9 30 B6
Binnie Rd. BH12 38 C2
Birch Av. BH23 33 G3
Birch Av. BH22 23 H1
Birch Clo. BH114 38 C4
Birch Clo. BH21 19 C5
Birch Clo. BH24 12 B4
Birch Dri. BH8 31 H3
Birch Gro. BH22 11 E4
Birch Gro. BH25 49 C6
Birch Rd. BH24 13 E3
Birchdale Rd. BH11 14 D4
Birchwood Clo. BH23 46 B4
Birchwood Rd. BH14 38 B4
Birchwood Rd. BH16 34 B3
Birchy Hill. SO41 54 C4
*Birds Hill Gdns,
 Birds Hill Rd. BH15 37 E3
Birds Hill Rd. BH15 37 E3
Birkdale Rd. BH18 20 A5
Birkdale Rd. BH18 20 A5
Bishop Clo. BH12 29 F5
Bishop Rd. BH9 30 C6
Bishops Clo. BH7 41 H1
Bishops Ct. BH24 8 D4
Bitterne Way. BH31 6 D3
Black Hill. BH31 6 D2
Blackberry La. BH23 45 E4
Blackbird Rd. BH17 34 E2
Blackbird Way. BH23 54 D1
Blackburn Rd. BH12 37 G1
Blackbush Rd. SO41 50 C3
Blackfield La. BH22 11 E3
Blackfield Rd. BH8 31 F2
Blackmoor Rd. BH31 6 F4
Blacksmith Clo. BH21 19 C6
Blackthorn Way. BH25 48 F3
Blackwater Dri. BH21 20 C3
Blair Av. BH14 37 H3

Blair Clo. BH25 48 A4
Blake Dene Rd. BH14 37 H6
Blake Hill Av. BH14 38 B6
Blake Hill Cres. BH14 37 H6
Blandford Rd. BH15 18 B2
Blandford Rd. BH15 35 D5
Blandford Rd Nth.
 BH16 34 A1
Blaney Way. BH21 19 C5
Blenheim Cres. SO41 55 A1
Blenheim Dri. BH23 45 G4
Blind La. BH21 14 B3
Bloomfield Av. BH9 30 B3
Bloxworth Rd. BH12 28 D4
Bluebell Clo. BH23 45 H2
Bluebell La. BH11 34 E1
Blyth Cl. BH23o 32 C2
Blythe Rd. BH21 19 D5
Blyths Wood Ct. BH25 49 B7
Bockhampton Rd,
 Bransgore. BH23 54 A2
Bockhampton Rd,
 Winkton. BH23 33 H1
Bodley Rd. BH13 53 E2
Bodorgan Rd. BH2 40 B4
Bodowen Clo. BH23 33 H5
Bodowen Rd. BH23 33 H5
Bognor Rd. BH18 19 F7
Boldre Clo. BH25 47 G5
Boldre Clo. BH12 28 C6
Boleyn Cres. BH9 31 E1
Bolton Clo. BH6 43 E5
Bolton Cres. BH22 17 H2
Bolton Rd. BH6 43 E5
Bond Av. BH22 11 E2
Bond Clo. SO41 54 B3
Bond Rd. BH15 37 E2
Bonham Rd. BH9 40 B1
Bonington Clo. BH23 44 D2
Border Dri. BH16 34 C4
Border Rd. BH16 34 C4
Boreham Rd. BH6 42 D3
Borley Rd. BH17 26 A5
Borthwick Rd. BH1 41 G3
Boscombe Cliff Rd.
 BH5 41 G5
Boscombe Grove Rd.
 BH1 41 F3
Boscombe Overcliff Dri.
 BH5 42 A5
Boscombe Prom. BH5 41 G5
Boscombe Rd. BH6 43 F6
Boscombe Spa Rd. BH5 41 F4
Bosley Clo. BH23 32 D4
Bosley Way. BH23 32 C4
Bosworth Mews. BH9 30 D1
Boulnois Av. BH14 38 C4
Boundary Dri. BH21 14 D3
Boundary La. BH24 12 A6
Boundary Rd. BH10 30 A4
Bountys La. BH12 38 C1
Bourne Av. BH2 5 B1
Bourne Clo. BH10 30 A1
Bourne Ct. BH21 14 A4
Bourne Valley Rd. BH12 39 E3
Bournemouth Central
 Business Park. BH1 41 E4
Bournemouth Rd. BH14 37 H3
Bournewood Dri. BH4 39 G3
Bourton Gdns. BH7 42 B1
Bouverie Clo. BH25 49 B6
Boveridge Gdns. BH9 30 D1
Bovington Clo. BH17 27 F3
Bowden Rd. BH12 28 B2
Bower Rd. BH8 31 E5
Bowland Rise. BH25 48 E4
Box Clo. BH17 26 B5
Boyd Rd. BH12 38 D1
Brabazon Dri. BH23 45 G3
Brabazon Rd. BH21 21 E1
Brabourne Av. BH22 17 E4
Bracken Clo. BH22 16 D2
Bracken Clo. BH24 12 C3
Bracken Glen. BH25 36 D2
Bracken Hill. BH13 39 E6
Bracken Rd. BH22 16 C1
Bracken Rd. BH6 42 C5
Bracken Way. BH23 42 D4
Brackendale Ct. BH21 7 A7
Brackenhill Rd. BH21 15 F2
Brackley Clo. BH23 25 G3
Bradburne Rd. BH2 5 B2
Bradford Rd. BH9 30 B4
Bradpole Rd. BH8 31 F4
Bradstock Clo. BH12 28 D5

Braemar Av. BH6 43 G5
Braemar Clo. BH6 43 G5
Braemar Dri. BH23 46 C4
Braeside Rd. BH24 12 C3
Braeside Rd. BH22 11 F3
Braidley Rd. BH2 5 C2
Brailswood Rd. BH15 36 D3
Bramble Ct. BH22 11 E4
Bramble La. BH23 47 E4
Bramble Way. BH23 54 C1
Bramley Rd. BH22 17 E2
Bramley Rd. BH10 23 E5
Brampton Rd. BH15 36 D1
Bramshaw Gdns. BH8 31 F3
Branch La. BH24 9 G4
Branders Clo. BH6 43 G4
Branders La. BH6 43 G4
Branksea Av. BH15 35 D8
Branksea Clo. BH15 35 E8
Branksome Clo. BH25 48 D4
Branksome Dene Rd.
 BH4 39 F5
Branksome Hill Rd. BH4 39 F2
Branksome Towers.
 BH13 53 H1
Branksome Wood Gdns.
 BH2 40 A4
Branksome Wood Rd.
 BH2 40 A4
Bransgore Gdns. BH23 54 C1
Branshaw Way. BH25 47 G4
Branwell Clo. BH23 33 E5
Branwood Clo. SO41 55 C3
Brassey Clo. BH9 30 C4
Brassey Rd. BH9 30 B4
Breamore Clo. BH25 47 H2
Brecon Clo. BH10 23 G5
Brecon Clo. BH25 48 E4
Bredy Clo. BH17 26 D3
Bremble Clo. BH12 28 B2
Brendon Clo. BH8 31 F4
Briar Clo. BH23 45 E4
Briar Clo. BH15 36 D2
Briar Way. BH21 15 G4
Briarswood Rd. BH16 34 C2
Brickyard La. BH21 18 A3
Brickyard La. BH23 16 C3
Bridge Approach.
 BH15 36 A6
Bridge Pl. BH10 23 D4
Bridge St. BH23 44 C4
Bridges Clo. BH22 11 F3
Bridgewater Rd. BH12 38 B1
Bridle Clo. BH16 34 D3
Bridle Cres. BH7 42 D1
Bridleway. BH21 15 H3
Bridleways. BH31 6 B2
Bridport Rd. BH31 6 C2
Bridport Rd. BH12 28 D4
Brierley Av. BH22 23 H1
Brierley Clo. BH10 30 A1
Brierley Rd. BH10 30 A1
Bright Rd. BH15 36 D1
Brightlands Av. BH6 43 F4
Brighton Rd. SO41 54 A3
Brinsons Clo. BH23 33 H4
Brisbane Rd. BH23 32 D5
Britannia Rd. BH14 37 F4
Britannia Way. BH23 45 G3
Brixey Clo. BH12 28 A5
Brixey Rd. BH12 27 H6
Broad Av. BH8 31 F5
Broad Mead Rd. BH21 7 C6
Broadfields Clo. SO41 51 E3
Broadhurst Av. BH10 30 A1
Broadlands Av. BH6 43 F4
Broadlands Clo. BH8 31 F3
Broadlands Clo. BH23 47 F3
Broadmayne Rd. BH12 28 D5
Brôadmoor Rd. BH21 19 B5
Broadshard Rd. BH24 8 D3
Broadshard La. BH24 8 D3
Broadstone Way. BH18 26 A3
Broadwater Av. BH1 37 H5
Broadway. BH6 43 H5
Broadway Gdns. BH21 14 C5
Broadway La. BH8 31 G5
Brockenhurst Rd. BH9 30 D4
Brockhills La. BH25 48 F3
Brockley Rd. BH10 29 H1
Brocks Pine. BH24 12 D4
Brog St. BH21 18 C3
Bronte Av. BH23 33 E4
Brook Av. BH25 48 C3
Brook Av Nth. BH25 48 C2

Brook Clo. BH10 29 F1
Brook Dri. BH31 6 E3
Brook La. BH23 54 B2
Brook La. BH21 19 B5
Brook Park Ind Est.
 BH21 15 E5
Brook Rd. BH21 14 D5
Brook Rd. BH10 23 E6
Brook Rd. BH12 37 H1
Brook Way. BH23 45 H3
Brookdale Clo. BH18 20 A6
Brookdale Farm. BH18 20 A6
Brooklyn Ct. BH25 48 B4
Brooks Clo. BH24 8 D6
Brookside Clo. BH23 54 B1
Brookside Rd. BH23 54 B1
Brookside Rd. BH21 15 E4
Brookside Way. BH23 46 D3
Broom Rd. BH12 27 H3
Broughton Av. BH10 30 A1
Broughton Clo. BH10 30 A1
Brownen Rd. BH9 30 C6
Browning Av. BH5 42 A4
Browning Rd. BH12 38 B1
Brownsea Rd. BH21 19 D5
Brownsea Clo. BH23 48 A4
Brownsea Rd. BH13 52 B6
Brownsea Vw Av.
 BH14 37 H6
Brownsea Vw Clo.
 BH14 37 H6
Brudenell Av. BH13 52 D2
Brudenell Rd. BH13 52 D3
Brunel Clo. BH31 6 F3
Brunes Way. BH22 17 F6
Brunstead Pl. BH12 39 F3
Brunstead Rd. BH12 39 E3
Bryanstone Rd. BH3 30 A6
Bryant Rd. BH12 29 E4
Bryony Clo. BH18 19 E8
Bub La. BH23 44 D4
Buccaneers Clo. BH13 44 D4
Buccleuch Rd. BH13 53 G1
Bucehayes Clo. BH23 46 D3
Buchanan Av. BH7 41 G2
Buckingham Rd. BH12 28 B6
Buckland Gro. BH23 46 B3
Buckland Rd. BH12 37 H2
Buckland Ter. BH12 38 A2
Bucklers Way. BH8 31 F2
Buckstone Clo. SO41 55 C3
Buckthorn Clo. BH17 Inset 19
Bugdens La. BH31 6 D2
Bulldowne Walk 54 B3
Bullfinch Clo. BH17 Inset 19
Bunting Rd. BH22 16 D1
Burbridge Clo. BH17 27 E5
Burcombe Av. BH24 9 G3
Burcombe Rd. BH10 23 E6
Burdock Clo. BH23 45 H1
Bure Clo. BH23 45 H4
Bure Haven Dri. BH23 45 F4
Bure Homage Gdns.
 BH23 45 G4
Bure Homage La. BH23 45 G4
Bure La. BH23 45 G5
Bure Park. BH23 45 H4
Bure Rd. BH23 45 H4
Burford Clo. BH23 32 C5
Burgess Clo. BH11 28 D1
Burleigh Rd. BH6 43 F1
Burley Clo. BH31 6 B2
Burley Rd,
 Bransgore. BH23 54 A2
Burley Rd. BH12 37 H1
Burley Rd,
 Winkton. BH23 33 H1
Burlington Arcade. BH1 5 D2
Burnaby Rd. BH4 39 F6
Burnbake Rd. BH31 6 C2
Burnbrae Rd. BH22 23 G1
Burnett Av. BH23 45 H4
Burnett Rd. BH23 43 F1
Burngate Rd. BH15 35 E7
Burnham Dri. BH8 31 E6
Burnham Rd. BH23 33 G4
Burnleigh Gdns. BH25 48 E3
Burns Rd. BH6 43 E5
Burnside. BH23 46 B5
Burnt House La. BH13 44 A4
Burntley Rd. BH6 43 E5
Burton Clo. BH24 12 C2
Burton Croft. BH23 33 G3
Burton Green. BH23 33 H4

Burton Hall. BH23 33 H3
Burton Hall Clo. BH23 33 H3
Burton Rd. BH23 44 D3
Burton Rd. BH13 39 E4
Burts Hill. BH21 14 B2
Bury Rd. BH13 38 D5
Bushell Rd. BH15 26 C6
Bushey Rd. BH8 30 D5
Bushmead Dri. BH24 12 C2
Bute Clo. BH23 47 E5
Butlers La. BH4 9 E3
Buttercup Dri. BH23 45 H1
Byron Clo. BH25 49 A6
Byron Rd. BH5 41 H4
Byron Rd. BH21 14 C3

Cabot La. BH17 26 A5
Cabot Way. BH25 48 B4
Cadhay Clo. BH25 47 H1
Cadnam Way. BH8 31 F3
Cadogan Rd. BH24 8 D5
Caesars Way. BH18 19 D7
Caird Av. BH25 48 D4
Cairns Clo. BH23 32 D6
Caister Dri. BH22 17 E2
Calder Rd. BH17 27 F4
Caledon Rd. BH14 37 H4
Caledonian Clo. BH23 45 H3
Calkin Clo. . BH23 33 F5
Calluna Rd. BH15 27 G4
Calmore Clo. BH8 31 E2
Calvin Rd. BH9 30 B5
Cambridge Gdns. BH23 33 E4
Cambridge Rd. BH2 5 A2
Camden Clo. BH9 30 C4
Camellia Clo. BH21 7 B7
Camellia Gdns. BH25 48 D4
Cameron Rd. BH23 44 D3
Cammel Rd. BH22 23 F1
Campbell Rd. BH1 41 G3
Campbell Rd. BH23 33 G3
Campion Gro. BH23 45 E4
Canberra Rd. BH23 32 D5
Candys Clo. BH21 18 E2
Candys La. BH21 18 D2
Canford Av. BH11 28 D3
Canford Bottom. BH21 15 G3
Canford Cliffs Av. BH14 38 B5
Canford Cliffs Rd. BH13 53 E1
Canford Cres. BH13 53 E3
Canford Gdns. BH10 29 E3
Canford Heath Rd.
 BH17 26 C3
Canford Magna. BH21 21 F1
Canford Rd. BH15 36 D3
Canford Rd. BH11 29 E4
Canford View Dri. BH21 15 G2
Canford Way. BH12 27 H2
Cannon Clo. BH18 26 A3
Cannon Hill Gdns.
 BH21 15 G1
Cannon Hill Rd. BH21 15 F2
Cannons Walk. SO41 51 E3
Canterbury Clo. BH22 11 F5
Canute Dri. BH23 54 C1
Capesthorne. BH23 45 G5
Capstone Pl. BH8 41 F2
Capstone Rd. BH8 40 D2
Caradon Pl. BH31 6 A1
Carbery Av. BH6 42 D4
Carbery Gdns. BH6 43 E4
Carbery Row. BH6 42 C4
Cardigan Rd. BH12 38 D3
Cardigan Rd. BH9 30 B6
Carey Rd. BH9 30 B3
Careys Rd. BH8 31 E2
Carisbrooke Cres. BH15 35 D6
Carisbrooke Way. BH23 46 C4
Carlton Av. BH25 47 G5
Carlton Gro. BH12 38 D2
Carlton Rd. BH1 41 E4
Carlyle Rd. BH6 42 D2
Carmel Clo. BH15 35 D7
Carnarvon Rd. BH1 41 G4
Carnegie Clo. BH12 38 B2
Caroline Av. BH23 45 E4
Caroline Rd. BH11 29 F2
Carradale. BH23 45 H2
Carrbridge Clo. BH3 29 G6
Carrbridge Gdns. BH3 29 G6
Carrbridge Rd. BH3 29 G6
Carrick Way. BH25 49 E5
Carrington Clo. SO41 51 F4
Carrington La. SO41 51 F4
Carroll Av. BH22 17 F3

59

Ingworth Rd. BH12 39 E2
Insley Cres. BH18 19 E6
Inveravon. BH23 45 F5
Inverclyde Rd. BH14 37 H3
Inverleigh Rd. BH6 42 D3
Inverness Rd. BH13 53 E2
Ipswich Rd. BH4 39 F3
Iris Rd. BH9 30 A5
Irvine Way. BH23 45 E2
Irving Rd. BH6 42 D4
Isaacs Clo. BH12 29 F5
Island View Av. BH23 45 G4
Island View Clo. SO41 51 F5
Island View Rd. BH25 47 G6
Ivamy Pl. BH11 28 D3
Ivor Rd. BH21 19 D7
Ivor Rd. BH15 36 A6
Ivy Clo. BH24 12 B4
Ivy La. BH24 8 C1
Ivy Rd. BH21 20 C3
Iwerne Clo. BH9 30 D2

Jackson Gdns. BH12 38 B1
Jackson Rd. BH12 38 B1
Jacobean Clo. BH23 47 E3
Jacobs Rd. BH15 35 D7
Jacqueline Rd. BH12 27 H5
James Rd. BH12 39 E2
Jameson Rd. BH9 30 A5
Janred Ct. BH25 49 A8
Jaundrells Clo. BH25 48 D4
Jays Ct. BH23 47 E5
Jefferson Av. BH1 41 F2
Jellicoe Clo. BH14 37 F2
Jellicoe Dri. BH23 45 F4
Jennings Rd. BH14 37 H5
Jephcote Rd. BH11 28 D1
Jersey Clo. BH12 28 B3
Jesmond Av. BH23 46 D5
Jessica Av. BH31 6 A1
Jessop Clo. BH10 30 B2
Jessopp Rd. BH21 15 G3
Jewell Rd. BH8 31 H4
Johnson Rd. BH21 16 C21
Johnston Rd. BH23 45 E4
Johnston Rd. BH15 26 D6
Jolliffe Av. BH15 36 D3
Jolliffe Rd. BH15 36 D3
Jordans La. SO41 54 C3
Jowitt Dri. BH25 49 B5
Joyce Dickson Clo.
BH24 9 E6
Joys Rd. BH21 7 B7
Jubilee Av. BH21 19 D5
Jubilee Clo. BH24 9 E4
Jubilee Cres. BH12 38 B2
Jubilee Rd. BH12 38 B2
Jubilee Rd. BH21 19 D5
Julia Clo. BH23 46 C4
Julians Rd. BH21 14 A4
Julyan Av. BH12 29 E4
Jumpers Av. BH23 32 D6
Jumpers Rd. BH23 32 D6
Junction Rd. BH16 35 D5
Junction Rd. BH9 30 B6
Juniper Clo. BH22 10 D6
Juniper Clo. BH21 7 B7
Jupiter Way. BH21 18 D4
Justin Gdns. BH10 23 H6

Kangaw Pl. BH15 35 D8
Katherine Chance Clo.
BH23 33 H3
Katterns Clo. BH23 32 D5
Keats Av. SO41 51 E4
Keeble Clo. BH10 23 G5
Keeble Cres. BH10 23 G5
Keeble Rd. BH10 23 G4
Keepers Hill. BH21 16 B4
Keighley Av. BH18 26 A3
Keith Rd. BH3 39 G1
Kellaway Rd. BH17 27 F4
Kelly Clo. BH17 27 F5
Kelsall Gdns. BH25 48 B4
Kemp Rd. BH9 30 A6
Ken Rd. BH6 43 E5
Kenilworth Clo. BH25 48 D4
Kennard Ct. BH25 48 B4
Kennard Rd. BH25 48 B3
Kennart Rd. BH17 26 B5
Kennington Rd. BH17 26 D5
Kensington Dri. BH2 39 H3
Kensington Pk. SO41 50 D4
Kent Rd. BH12 38 C1
Kenyon Clo. BH15 27 E6

Kenyon Rd. BH15 27 E6
Keppel Clo. BH24 9 E4
Kerley Rd. BH2 5 C3
Kestrel Clo. BH22 16 D1
Kestrel Clo. BH16 34 B2
Kestrel Ct. BH24 8 C4
Kestrel Dri. BH23 45 F4
Keswick Rd. BH5 42 A4
Keswick Rd. BH25 48 D2
Keswick Way. BH31 6 B2
Keyes Clo. BH23 45 F4
Keyes Clo. BH12 28 D4
Keyhaven Rd. SO41 51 F5
Keysworth Av. BH25 49 B7
Keysworth Rd. BH16 35 C5
Khyber Rd. BH12 38 B2
Kilmarnock Rd. BH9 30 B5
Kilmington Way. BH23 46 C4
Kiln Clo. BH21 19 B7
Kimber Rd. BH11 28 D1
Kimberley Clo. BH23 32 D6
Kimberley Rd. BH14 37 G4
Kimberley Rd. BH6 42 C3
Kimmeridge Av. BH12 27 H5
King Clo. BH24 9 E4
King Edward Av. BH9 30 B3
King George Av. BH9 30 B4
King John Av. BH11 22 A5
King John Clo. BH11 22 A5
King Richard Dri. BH11 22 A6
King St. BH21 14 B4
Kingcup Clo. BH18 Inset 19
Kingfisher Clo. BH6 43 E3
Kingfisher Clo. BH22 11 F4
Kingfisher Way. BH24 45 F5
Kingfisher Way. BH24 9 E2
Kingland Cres. BH15 36 C5
Kingland Rd. BH15 36 C4
Kings Arms La. BH24 8 B5
Kings Arms Row. BH24 8 B5
Kings Av. BH23 43 F2
Kings Av. BH14 38 B5
Kings Clo. BH22 11 E5
Kings Cres. BH14 38 C5
Kings Farm La. SO41 55 D2
Kings Park Central Dri.
BH7 41 G2
Kings Park Dri. BH7 41 G2
Kings Park Rd. BH7 41 G2
Kings Rd. BH25 48 E3
Kings Rd. BH3 40 C1
Kingsbere Av. BH10 29 F3
Kingsbere Rd. BH15 36 D2
Kingsbridge Rd. BH14 37 H4
Kingsbury La. BH24 8 B5
Kingsfield. BH24 8 C5
Kingsley Av. BH6 43 G5
Kingsley Clo. BH6 43 G5
Kingsmill Rd. BH17 27 E5
Kingston Rd. BH15 36, D3
Kingsway Clo. BH23 33 E5
Kingsway. BH22 16 D1
Kingswell Clo. BH10 29 G2
Kingswell Gdns. BH10 29 F2
Kingswell Gro. BH10 29 F2
Kingswell Rd. BH10 29 F2
Kinross Rd. BH3 40 A2
Kinsbourne Av. BH10 29 H3
Kinson Av. BH15 27 G6
Kinson Rd. BH10 23 F5
Kinson Park Rd. BH10 23 F4
Kinson Rd. BH10 23 E5
Kipling Rd. BH14 37 G2
Kirby Clo. BH15 37 F1
Kirby Way. BH6 42 D5
Kirkham Av. BH23 33 G3
Kirkway. BH18 26 B1
Kitchener Cres. BH17 26 B3
Kitchens Clo. SO41 54 B3
Kitscroft Rd. BH10 23 F5
Kittiwake Clo. BH6 42 D2
Kitwalls Clo. SO41 51 E3
Kivernell Rd. SO41 50 D4
Kiwi Clo. BH15 37 E4
Knapp Clo. BH23 33 F6
Knapp Mill Av. BH23 33 E6
Knighton Heath Clo.
BH11 22 B6
Knighton Heath Ind Est.
BH11 28 C2
Knighton Heath Rd.
BH11 22 B6
Knighton La. BH21 22 A4
Knighton Pk. BH25 47 H4
Knights Rd. BH11 22 A6

*Knightstone Gro
Moorlands Rd. BH22 11 E4
Knightwood Clo. BH23 46 B5
Knobcrook Rd. BH21 14 B3
Knole Gdns. BH1 41 F4
Knole Rd. BH1 41 F3
Knole Rd. BH24 12 D3
Knoll La. BH21 18 A4
Knowland Dri. SO41 51 E3
Knowles Clo. BH23 44 D3
Knowlton Gdns. BH9 30 C2
Knowlton Rd. BH17 27 F3
Knyveton Rd. BH1 41 E4
Kyrchil La. BH21 15 E2
Kyrchil Way. BH21 15 E2

Labrador Dri. BH15 36 D6
Laburnum Clo. BH22 16 D2
Laburnum Clo. BH31 6 F3
Laburnum Dri. SO41 55 E3
Lacey Cres. BH15 37 G1
Lacy Clo. BH21 14 C3
Lacy Dri. BH21 14 C3
Ladysmith Clo. BH23 44 D3
Lagado Clo. BH14 52 D1
Lagland St. BH15 36 C5
Lagoon Rd. BH14 52 B1
Laidlaw Clo. BH12 29 F5
Lake Av. BH15 35 D8
Lake Cres. BH15 35 E6
Lake Dri. BH15 35 C7
Lake Grove Rd. BH25 48 B3
Lake Rd. BH15 35 D8
Lake Rd. BH11 23 E5
Lake Rd. BH31 6 D3
Lakeside. BH24 9 E6
Lakeside Rd. BH13 53 G1
Lakeview Dri. BH24 9 F6
Lakewood Rd. BH23 46 C4
Lambs Clo. BH17 26 C3
Lambsgreen La. BH21 18 E2
Lampton Gdns. BH9 30 B4
Lancaster Clo. BH18 19 E6
Lancaster Clo. BH23 45 H3
Lancaster Dri. BH18 19 E6
Lancaster Dri. BH31 6 B2
Lancaster Rd. BH21 16 C1
Lancer Clo. BH23 43 F1
Lander Clo. BH15 36 D5
Landford Gdns. BH8 31 F3
Landford Way. BH8 31 E3
Landseer Rd. BH4 39 F4
Langdon Rd. BH14 38 B5
Langley Chase. BH24 13 D2
Langley Rd. BH14 38 C3
Langley Rd. BH23 46 B3
Langside Av. BH12 29 E5
Langton Clo. BH25 49 C6
Langton Rd. BH7 41 H3
Lansdowne Cres. BH1 5 F1
Lansdowne Gdns. BH1 43 D4
Lansdowne Rd. BH1 40 C3
Lansdowne Rd Sth. BH1 5 F1
Lapwing Rd. BH17 15 F1
Lara Clo. BH8 31 E2
Larch Clo. SO41 55 B1
Larch Clo. BH24 13 E3
Larch Clo. BH17 34 E1
Larch Way. BH22 17 E1
Lark Rd. BH23 45 G4
Larks Rise. BH22 16 D1
Larkshill Av. BH9 30 D3
Larkshill Clo. BH25 48 C3
Lascelles Rd. BH7 42 B3
Latch Farm Av. BH23 33 F6
Latimer Rd. BH9 30 B6
Latimers Clo. BH23 46 C3
Laundry La. SO41 51 F5
Laurel Clo. BH21 19 C5
Laurel Clo. BH23 46 A4
Laurel Clo. SO41 55 A1
Laurel Clo. BH24 12 C4
Laurel Dri. BH18 20 B6
Laurel Gdns. BH18 20 B6
Laurel La. BH24 12 C4
Lavender Clo. BH9 6 F3
Lavender Dri. BH8 31 F2
Lavender Rd. SO41 55 A1
Lavender Way. BH18 19 D8
Lavinia Rd. BH12 27 H5
Lawford Rd. BH9 30 C2
Lawn Clo. SO41 51 F4
Lawn Rd. SO41 51 F4
Lawns Clo. BH21 15 H3
Lawns Rd. BH21 15 G3
Lawrence Ct. BH8 41 E2

Lawrence Dri. BH13 38 C6
Lawrence Rd. BH21 9 F2
Lawson Rd. BH12 37 H1
Layard Dri. BH21 20 D2
Layton Rd. BH23 44 D3
Le Patourel Clo. BH23 44 D3
Lea Way. BH11 22 B4
Leamington Rd. BH9 30 C6
Leaphill Rd. BH7 42 B3
Learoyd Rd. BH17 27 E5
Lechlade Gdns. BH7 42 B1
Ledbury Rd. BH23 45 F4
Ledgard Clo. BH14 37 H3
Leedam Rd. BH10 23 F6
Leeson Dri. BH22 16 D1
Leeson Rd. BH7 41 G1
Legg La. BH21 14 C4
Legion Clo. BH15 35 E7
Legion Rd. BH15 35 E7
Leicester Rd. BH13 38 C3
Leigh Gdns. BH21 14 D5
Leigh La. BH21 15 E4
Leigh Rd. BH25 48 C3
Leigh Rd. BH21 14 C4
Leigham Vale Rd. BH6 42 D4
Lentham Clo. BH17 26 D3
Leslie Rd. BH14 37 F4
Leslie Rd. BH9 30 A6
Leven Av. BH4 39 G2
Leven Clo. BH4 39 H3
Levets La. BH15 36 B5
Lewens Clo. BH21 14 C4
Lewens La. BH21 14 C4
Lewesdon Dri. BH18 19 E7
Leybourne Av. BH10 23 F5
Leybourne Clo. BH10 23 F5
Leydene Av. BH8 31 G5
Leydene Clo. BH8 31 G5
Leyland Rd. BH12 28 C3
Leyside. BH23 45 F4
Library Rd. BH21 38 C2
Library Rd. BH22 17 F3
Library Rd. BH9 30 C6
Lilac Clo. BH24 8 D4
Lilliput Clo. BH14 52 C1
Lilliput Rd. BH14 52 C1
Lime Clo. BH15 37 F1
Lime Gro. SO41 55 B4
Limited Rd. BH9 30 C4
Linbrook Dri. BH24 9 E2
Lincoln Av. BH1 41 F2
Lincoln Av. BH23 33 E4
Lincoln Rd. BH12 28 B6
Lindbergh Rd. BH21 16 C1
Linden Clo. BH22 23 F1
Linden Gdns. BH24 8 C4
Linden Rd. BH22 23 F1
Linden Rd. BH9 31 B2
Linden Rd. BH12 37 H1
Lindsay Rd. BH13 38 D3
Lineside. BH23 33 H6
Linford Clo. BH25 48 C3
Linford Rd. BH24 9 E3
Ling Rd. BH12 27 G4
Lingdale Rd. BH6 42 D3
Lingwood Av. BH23 45 E4
Linhorns La. BH25 48 C2
Link Rise. BH21 19 D6
Link Rd. BH24 9 E3
Links Dri. BH23 32 C5
Links Rd. BH14 38 B5
Links View Av. BH14 38 C5
Linside Av. BH8 31 G5
Linmead Dri. BH11 22 D5
Linnet Clo. BH24 9 F6
Linnet Ct. BH25 48 B4
Linnet Rd. BH17 34 E1
Linthorpe Rd. BH15 37 E3
Linwood Rd. BH9 30 C6
Lionheart Clo. BH11 22 A6
Lions Hill Way. BH24 12 A3
Lions La. BH24 12 B3
Lions Wood. BH24 12 C3
Litchford Rd. BH25 48 E3
Little Barrs Dri. BH25 48 E3
Little Burn. SO41 54 B3
Little Croft Rd. BH12 37 G1
Little Forest Rd. BH4 39 H2
Little Lonnen. BH21 15 F1
Littlecroft Av. BH9 30 D3
Littledown Av. BH7 41 G1
Littledown Dri. BH7 41 G1
Littlemead Clo. BH17 26 A5
Littlemoor Av. BH11 28 C1
Little Barrs Dri. BH23 44 D3
Livingstone Rd. BH23 44 D3

Livingstone Rd. BH5 42 B4
Livingstone Rd. BH12 37 H1
Livingstone Rd. BH21 14 D5
Llewellin Clo. BH16 34 C2
Loch Rd. BH14 38 C2
Locksley Dri. BH22 17 E6
Lockyers Dri. BH22 17 H2
Lockyers Rd. BH21 18 D3
Loders Clo. BH17 26 D1
Lodge Clo. BH14 38 C3
Lodge Ct. BH14 38 C3
Lodge Rd. BH23 32 C6
Loewy Cres. BH12 28 B3
Lombard Av. BH6 42 D4
Lombardy Clo. BH31 6 E2
Lone Pine Dri. BH22 17 G6
Lone Pine Way. BH22 17 G6
Long Barrow Clo. BH8 31 H5
Long La. BH21 14 D1
Long Rd. BH10 23 F6
Longacre Dri. BH22 17 E5
Longespee Rd. BH21 20 D2
Longfield Dri. BH11 22 D5
Longfield Dri. BH22 23 G2
Longfield Rd. SO41 55 C2
Longfleet Rd. BH15 36 C4
Longleat Gdns. BH25 47 H2
Longmeadow La. BH16 34 E2
Lonnen Rd. BH21 15 E2
Lonnen Wood Clo.
BH21 15 F1
Lonsdale Rd. BH3 40 B1
Lord Clo. BH17 27 F5
Lorne Park Rd. BH1 5 E1
Lorraine Av. BH23 33 H3
Love La. SO41 51 E4
Lower Ashley Rd. BH25 48 F4
Lower Blandford Rd.
BH18 26 B1
Lower Common Rd.
BH21 7 D8
Lower Golf Links Rd.
BH18 20 A5
Lowther Gdns. BH8 41 E3
Lowther Rd. BH8 40 C2
Lucas Rd. BH12 38 A1
Lucas Rd. BH15 36 B6
Lucerne Av. BH6 42 D4
Lucerne Rd. SO41 51 E5
Luckham Clo. BH9 30 D4
Luckham Rd. BH9 30 D4
Luckham Rd East. BH9 30 D4
Lulworth Av. BH15 35 D8
Lulworth Clo. BH15 35 D8
Lulworth Cres. BH15 35 D8
Lumby Dri. BH24 9 E4
Luscombe Rd. BH14 38 B5
Luther Rd. BH9 30 B5
Lydford Gdns. BH11 29 E2
Lydford Rd. BH11 29 E2
Lydgate. SO41 50 B4
Lydlinch Clo. BH22 23 G2
Lydwell Clo. BH11 22 C5
Lyell Rd. BH12 38 B2
Lyme Cres. BH23 46 C5
Lymefield. SO41 51 F3
Lymington Rd. BH25 49 B6
Lymington Rd,
Everton. SO41 55 C4
Lymington Rd. BH23 46 A5
Lymington Rd, Milford-
on-Sea. SO41 51 E3
Lymore La,
Everton. SO41 55 C4
Lymore La, Milford-
on-Sea. SO41 51 F1
Lymore Valley. SO41 51 F2
Lyndale Clo. SO41 51 F4
Lyndhurst Rd. BH23 45 G2
Lynes La. BH24 8 B5
Lynn Rd. BH17 27 F4
Lynric Clo. BH25 49 B7
Lynton Cres. BH23 32 C3
Lynwood Clo. BH22 17 F2
Lynwood Dri. BH21 20 D2
Lyon Av. BH25 48 D4
Lyon Rd. BH12 28 C3
Lysander Clo. BH23 45 H3
Lystra Rd. BH9 30 C5
Lytchett Dri. BH18 26 A2
Lytchett Way. BH16 34 B3
Lytham Rd. BH18 26 A2
Lytton Rd. BH1 41 E3

Mabey Av. BH10 29 G2
MacAndrew Rd. BH3 53 D4

Macaulay Rd. BH18 26 B1
Maclaren Rd. BH9 30 B3
Maclean Rd. BH11 28 D2
Madeira Rd. BH1 5 E1
Madeira Rd. BH14 38 B2
Madeline Clo. BH12 27 H6
Madeline Cres. BH12 27 H6
Madison Av. BH1 41 F2
Magdalen La. BH23 43 G2
Magna Clo. BH11 22 C4
Magna Gdns. BH11 22 B4
Magna Rd. BH21 21 F2
Magnolia Clo. BH6 43 G4
Magnolia Clo. BH31 6 F3
Magpie Clo. BH8 31 E3
Magpie Gro. BH25 49 B5
Mags Barrow. BH22 23 H1
Maidment Clo. BH11 28 C1
Malan Clo. BH17 27 E5
Malcomb Clo. BH6 43 G6
Mallard Clo. BH8 31 E5
Mallard Clo. SO41 55 C1
Mallard Clo. BH23 45 F4
Mallard Rd. BH8 31 E5
Mallard Rd. BH21 15 F1
Mallory Clo. BH23 45 F2
Mallow Clo. BH18 19 E8
Mallow Clo. BH23 45 H2
Malmesbury Pk Pl. BH8 41 E3
Malmesbury Pk Rd.
  BH8 40 D2
Malmesbury Rd. BH24 12 C4
Maloren Way. BH22 11 G5
Malvern Clo. BH9 30 B3
Malvern Rd. BH9 30 B3
Manchester Rd. SO41 54 B3
Mandale Clo. BH11 29 E1
Mandale Rd. BH11 28 D2
Manderley. SO41 51 E5
Manning Av. BH23 46 A4
Mannings Heath Rd.
  BH12 27 H3
Mannington Way. BH22 10 D4
Manor Av. BH12 28 A4
Manor Clo. BH22 17 F3
Manor Clo. SO41 51 E3
Manor Ct. BH24 8 C4
Manor Farm Clo. BH25 49 B6
Manor Farm Rd. BH10 23 E4
Manor Gdns. BH24 8 C4
Manor Gdns. BH31 6 C1
Manor La. BH31 6 C3
Manor Pk. BH1 36 B2
Manor Rd. BH1 41 E5
Manor Rd. BH23 43 G2
Manor Rd. SO41 51 E3
Manor Rd. BH25 48 C4
Manor Rd. BH24 8 C4
Manor Rd. BH31 6 C1
Manor Way. BH31 6 C1
Mansel Clo. BH12 29 G5
Mansfield Av. BH11 37 H3
Mansfield Clo. BH22 23 G1
Mansfield Clo. BH14 37 H3
Mansfield Clo. BH14 37 H3
Mansfield Rd. BH9 30 A5
Mansfield Rd. BH24 8 C5
Manton Clo. BH15 35 E6
Manton Rd. BH15 35 E6
Maple Clo. BH25 49 D7
Maple Clo. BH23 46 C5
Maple Dri. BH22 17 E1
Maple Rd. BH15 36 D4
Maple Rd. BH9 30 A5
Mapperton Clo. BH17 27 F3
Marabout Clo. BH23 44 D3
Marchwood Rd. BH10 29 G1
Marden Ho. SO41 50 C4
Margards La. BH31 6 A2
Marian Clo. BH21 19 B7
Marian Rd. BH21 19 B7
Marianne Rd. BH21 15 F2
Marianne Rd. BH12 29 F5
Marie Clo. BH12 28 B6
Marina Clo. BH5 41 G5
Marina Dri. BH14 37 G6
*Marina View,
  Willow Dri. BH23 43 G3
Marine Dri East. BH25 49 B8
Marine Dri West. BH25 49 A8
Marine Rd. BH6 42 D5
Market Clo. BH15 36 B5
Market Pl. BH24 8 B5
Market St. BH15 36 B5
Market Way. BH21 14 C5
Markham Av. BH10 23 G4

Markham Clo. BH10 23 G4
Markham Rd. BH9 30 B6
Marks La. BH25 48 C1
Marks Rd. BH9 30 B3
Marlborough Pl. BH21 14 C3
Marlborough Rd. BH14 37 H3
Marlborough Rd. BH4 39 G4
Marley Av. BH25 48 A3
Marley Clo. BH25 48 A4
Marline Rd. BH12 38 C1
Marlott Rd. BH15 36 C2
Marlow Dri. BH23 32 C3
Marlpit Dri. BH23 46 D3
Marmion Grn. BH23 45 E3
Marnhull Rd. BH15 36 D3
Marpet Clo. BH10 22 C5
Marquis Way. BH11 22 A6
Marryat Ct. BH25 47 E5
Marryat Rd. BH25 48 B4
Marsh Ditch. BH23 43 G3
Marsh La,
  Fairmile. BH23 33 E4
Marsh La,
  Purewell. BH23 44 D4
Marsh La. BH16 34 A2
Marshall Rd. BH17 26 B3
Marshfield. BH21 15 E2
Marshwood Av. BH17 27 E2
Marston Clo. BH25 48 D2
Marston Rd. BH25 48 D2
Marston Rd. BH15 36 B5
Marstone Gro. BH23 46 B3
Martello Park. BH13 53 F2
Martello Rd. BH13 38 C6
Martello Rd Sth. BH13 53 F1
Martells. BH25 49 D7
Martin Clo. BH17 34 F2
Martin Rd. BH12 38 C2
Martindale Av. BH15 15 G4
Martingale Clo. BH16 34 D3
Martins Clo. BH22 17 F2
Martins Dri. BH22 17 F2
Martins Hill Clo. BH23 33 H5
Martins Hill La. BH23 33 H5
Martins Way. BH22 17 F2
Marwell Clo. BH7 42 A2
Mary La. BH22 11 E4
Maryland Gdns. SO41 50 C4
Maryland Rd. BH16 35 C5
Masterson Clo. BH23 44 D3
Matchams La. BH23 25 H1
Matlock Rd. BH22 17 E6
Maundeville Cres.
  BH23 32 C6
Maundeville Rd. BH23 32 C6
Maureen Clo. BH12 27 H5
Maurice Rd. BH8 31 E6
Mavis Rd. BH9 30 D4
Maxwell Rd. BH13 53 F2
Maxwell Rd. BH18 19 D8
Maxwell Rd. BH9 30 B6
May Gdns. BH23 47 E3
May Gdns. BH11 28 C1
Mayfair Gdns. BH11 22 D6
Mayfield Av. BH14 38 C4
Mayfield Clo. BH22 17 E2
Mayfield Dri. BH22 17 E2
Mayfield Rd. BH9 30 B4
Mayfield Way. BH22 17 E3
Mayford Rd. BH12 39 F1
McIntyre Rd. BH23 25 F3
McKinley Rd. BH4 39 G5
McWilliam Clo. BH12 29 F5
McWilliam Rd. BH9 30 B3
Mead Clo. BH18 26 A3
Mead End Rd. SO41 54 A3
Meadow Bank. BH16 34 C2
Meadow Clo. BH24 8 D3
Meadow Clo. BH23 54 B2
Meadow Ct Clo. BH9 30 B3
Meadow Farm La. BH21 18 D3
Meadow Gro. BH31 6 E3
Meadow La. BH23 33 H4
Meadow Rise. BH18 19 E6
Meadow Rd. BH25 48 D3
Meadow Vw Rd. BH11 28 C1
Meadow Way. BH25 49 C8
Meadow West. BH25 48 D4
Meadow Way. BH31 6 D3
Meadowland. BH23 45 E4
Meadows Clo. BH16 34 C2
Meadows Dri. BH16 34 C2
Meadowsweet Rd.
  BH17 34 E1

Medina Way. BH23 46 A4
Medlar Clo. BH23 33 H5
Medway Rd. BH22 17 H4
Meeting House La. BH24 8 B5
Melbourne Rd. BH8 41 F2
Melbourne Rd. BH23 32 D5
Melbury Av. BH12 28 C5
Melbury Clo. BH22 17 E4
Mellstock Rd. BH15 36 C2
Melrose Ct. BH25 48 E4
Melverley Gdns. BH21 14 C3
Melville Gdns. BH8 30 A5
Melville Rd. BH9 30 A5
Mendip Clo. BH25 49 D5
Mendip Rd. BH31 6 C2
Mentone Rd. BH14 37 G4
Meon Rd. BH7 42 B2
Meredith Clo. BH23 44 D3
Meriden Clo. BH13 53 F2
Merino Way. BH22 11 F5
Merlewood Clo. BH2 40 B3
Merley Dri. BH23 46 D4
Merley Gdns. BH21 20 C2
Merley La. BH21 20 C2
Merley Park Rd. BH21 20 A4
Merley Ways. BH21 14 C6
Merlin Clo. BH24 9 F6
Merlin Way. BH23 45 G5
Merriefield Av. BH18 20 B5
Merriefield Clo. BH18 20 B5
Merriefield Dri. BH18 20 B5
Merrifield. BH21 14 D1
Merritown La. BH23 25 E4
Merrivale Av. BH6 43 E4
Merrow Av. BH12 39 F1
Merryfield Clo. BH23 54 B2
Merryfield La. BH10 29 G1
Merryweather Est. BH24 9 E4
Merton Gro. BH24 8 C4
Methuen Clo. BH8 41 E3
Methuen Rd. BH8 40 D3
Methuen Rd. BH17 26 C3
Meyrick Clo. BH23 54 B2
Meyrick Park Cres. BH3 40 B2
Meyrick Rd. BH1 40 D5
Michelgrove Rd. BH5 41 G5
Michelmersh Grn. BH8 31 F3
Mickleham Clo. BH12 29 F5
Middle La. BH24 8 C5
Middle Rd. BH10 23 E6
Middle Rd. BH15 36 D1
Middle Rd. SO41 54 B3
Middlebere Cres. BH16 35 C5
Middlehill Dri. BH21 15 G2
Middlehill Rd. BH21 15 E2
Middleton Rd. BH24 8 D4
Middleton Rd. BH9 30 A3
Midland Rd. BH9 30 B5
Midwood Av. BH8 31 G4
Milborne Cres. BH12 28 C5
Milburn Rd. BH22 17 E2
Milestone Rd. BH15 36 C1
Milford Clo. BH22 11 G4
Milford Ct. SO41 51 E4
Milford Cres. SO41 51 E4
Milford Dri. BH11 22 C5
Milford Rd. BH25 49 D6
Milford Rd. SO41 55 C4
Milford Trading Est.
  SO41 51 F5
Mill Hill Clo. BH14 37 G4
Mill La,
  Highcliffe. BH23 47 E4
Mill La, Hurn. BH23 25 H5
Mill La. BH14 37 G4
Mill La. BH21 14 B4
Mill Meadow. SO41 50 D4
Mill Rd. BH23 33 F6
Mill Rd. BH8 31 F2
Mill St. BH21 18 A2
Millburn Clo. BH4 39 F3
Millburn Rd. BH4 39 F3
Miller Clo. BH25 48 E3
Miller Rd. BH23 44 D3
Millfield. BH17 26 A5
Millhams Clo. BH10 23 E4
Millhams Dri. BH10 23 E4
Millhams Rd. BH10 22 D4
Millhams St. BH23 44 A4
Millstream Clo. BH17 26 A5
Millstream Clo. BH21 14 B4
Millyford Clo. BH25 47 G5
Milne Rd. BH17 26 B3
Milner Rd. BH4 39 G5
Milton Clo. BH14 38 B4
Milton Gro. BH25 49 D5

Milton Mead. BH25 49 B5
Milton Rd. BH8 40 C3
Milton Rd. BH14 38 B4
Milton Rd. BH21 14 B3
Milverton Clo. BH23 46 C5
Mimosa Av. BH21 20 D2
Minstead Rd. BH10 29 G1
Minster View. BH21 14 C3
Minster Way. BH16 34 B2
Minterne Rd. BH14 52 C2
Minterne Rd. BH9 30 C4
Minterne Rd. BH23 45 C7
Mission Rd. BH18 26 A2
Mitchell Clo. BH25 49 C6
Mitchell Rd. BH17 27 E5
Mitchell Rd. BH21 16 C1
Moat La. BH25 49 B6
Moffat Rd. BH23 44 D3
Molefields. SO41 51 E4
Molyneaux Rd. BH25 48 E4
Moneyfly Rd. BH31 6 E2
Monks Dri. BH22 11 H6
Monks Way. BH11 22 A6
Monkshood Clo. BH23 45 H1
Monkswell Grn. BH23 44 C3
Monkton Clo. BH22 17 F2
Monkton Cres. BH12 28 C5
Monkworthy Dri. BH24 12 D2
Monmouth Clo. BH31 6 E4
Monmouth Dri. BH31 6 E3
Monsal Av. BH22 17 E5
Montacute Way. BH21 20 D3
Montagu Rd. BH23 47 E5
Montague Rd. BH5 42 A3
Monteray Dri. SO41 55 B1
Montgomery Av. BH11 29 F1
Montrose Clo. BH31 6 C2
Montrose Dri. BH10 29 F3
Moonrakers Way. BH23 46 B4
Moor Rd. BH18 20 A6
Moor View Rd. BH15 27 E6
Moorcroft Av. BH23 33 H4
Moordown Clo. BH9 30 B2
Moore Av. BH11 29 E1
Moore Clo. BH25 49 B6
Moorfield Gro. BH9 30 B4
Moorfields Rd. BH13 53 F1
Moorland Av. BH25 49 B6
Moorland Cres. BH16 34 B3
Moorland Gate. BH24 8 C6
Moorland Rd. BH1 41 F4
Moorland Way. BH16 34 B3
Moorlands Rise. BH22 11 F3
Moorlands Rd. BH31 6 C1
Moorlands Rd. BH22 11 E4
Moors Clo. BH23 25 H4
Moorside Clo. BH11 29 F1
Moorside Rd. BH21 19 C6
Moorside Rd. BH11 29 E2
Moorside Rd. BH22 11 E4
Moorvale Rd. BH9 30 C4
Morant Rd. BH24 8 D2
Morden Av. BH22 17 E5
Morden Rd. BH9 30 A4
Moreton Rd. BH9 30 D1
Morley Clo. BH5 42 B4
Morley Rd. BH5 42 B4
Mornish Rd. BH13 38 D5
Morris Rd. BH17 26 D5
Morrison Av. BH12 38 D1
Mortimer Clo. BH23 45 G4
Mortimer Rd. BH8 31 G4
Mossley Av. BH12 28 D4
Motcombe Rd. BH13 39 E5
Mount Av. BH25 49 C6
Mount Clo. BH25 49 C6
Mount Grace Dri. BH14 52 D2
Mount Pleasant Dri.
  BH23 54 C1
Mount Pleasant Dri.
  BH8 31 G4
Mount Pleasant La.
  BH24 8 C4
Mount Pleasant Rd.
  BH15 36 D4
Mount Rd. BH11 29 E1
Mount Rd. BH14 37 G2
Mount Stuart Rd. BH5 41 G5
Mountbatten Clo. BH23 45 F5
Mountbatten Dri. BH22 17 E4
Mountbatten Gdns.
  BH8 31 H4
Mountbatten Rd. BH4 39 E5
Mountjoy Clo. BH21 21 F1
Mude Gdns. BH23 45 F5
Mudeford. BH23 45 E5

Mudeford Green Clo.
  BH23 45 F5
Mudeford La. BH23 44 D4
Mulberry Gro. SO41 55 C4
Mullins Clo. BH12 29 G4
Munster Rd. BH14 38 B4
Murley Rd. BH9 30 C5
Muscliff La. BH9 30 C2
Muscliffe Rd. BH9 30 B5
Myrtle Clo. SO41 55 B1
Myrtle Rd. BH8 41 F2
Nada Rd. BH23 46 A3
Nairn Rd. BH3 40 B2
Nairn Rd. BH13 53 E2
Naish Rd. BH25 47 G5
Namu Rd. BH9 30 A5
Nansen Av. BH15 36 D2
Napier Rd. BH15 35 C7
Narrow La. BH24 9 F3
Naseby Rd. BH9 30 C4
Nathan Gdns. BH15 35 D6
Nea Clo. BH23 46 B4
Nea Rd. BH23 46 B5
Neacroft Clo. BH25 47 G5
Needles Point. SO41 51 E5
Nelson Clo. BH25 48 B4
Nelson Dri. BH23 45 F4
Nelson Rd. BH4 39 E3
Netherhall Gdns. BH4 39 G4
Netley Clo. BH15 27 F6
Nettleton Clo. BH17 27 E5
New Borough Rd.
  BH21 14 C5
New Harbour Rd. BH15 36 B6
New Harbour Rd West.
  BH15 36 A6
New La. SO41 55 A5
New La. BH25 48 A1
New Merriefield. BH21 15 E1
New Orchard. BH15 36 B5
New Park Rd. BH6 42 C4
New Quay Rd. BH15 36 A6
New Rd. BH12 38 B1
New Rd. BH22 17 F4
New Rd. SO41 51 H5
New Rd. BH10 23 G4
New St. BH15 36 B5
New St. BH24 8 C6
New Valley Rd. SO41 50 D4
Newbury Dri. BH10 29 G3
Newcombe Rd. BH6 43 E3
Newcombe Rd. BH22 11 E4
Newcroft Gdns. BH23 43 G1
Newfields Business Pk.
  BH17 26 D4
Newfoundland Dri.
  BH15 36 C5
Newlands Rd. BH23 45 F3
Newlands Rd. BH25 49 D5
Newlands Rd. BH7 42 A2
Newlands Way. BH18 19 B8
Newlyn Way. BH12 28 C6
Newmans La. BH22 10 D1
Newmorton Rd. BH9 30 C1
Newstead Rd. BH6 42 D5
Newton Rd. BH25 49 D6
Newton Rd. BH13 53 E1
Newtown Business Pk.
  BH12 27 G5
Newtown La. BH21 18 D4
Newtown La. BH31 6 C3
Newtown Rd. BH31 6 D2
Nicholas Clo. BH23 47 E3
Nicholas Gdns. BH10 29 G3
Nicholson Clo. BH17 27 E5
Nightingale Clo. BH31 6 D3
Nightjar Clo. BH17 34 E2
Nimrod Way. BH21 16 B2
Noble Clo. BH11 28 D3
Noel Rd. BH10 29 F3
Noon Gdns. BH31 6 E1
Noon Hill Dri. BH31 6 E2
Noon Hill Rd. BH31 6 E2
Norcliffe Clo. BH11 29 F2
Norfolk Av. BH23 32 D5
Norleywood. BH23 46 C5
Norman Av. BH12 38 D1
Norman Gdns. BH12 38 D1
Normandy Clo. SO41 54 A3
Normandy Dri. BH23 44 D3
Normandy Dri. BH1 5 E1
Normandy Way. BH15 35 D7
Normanhurst Av. BH8 31 F5
Normanton Clo. BH23 32 D5
Norris Clo. BH24 12 C3
Norris Gdns. BH25 49 C5

*Quarterjack Mews,
East St. BH21 14 B4
Quay Rd. BH3 44 B4
Quayle Dri. BH11 22 C5
Queen Anne Dri. BH21 20 C3
Queen Mary Av. BH9 30 B4
Queens Av. BH23 44 B5
Queens Clo. BH4 39 G4
Queens Clo. BH22 11 E5
Queens Gdns. BH2 39 H3
Queens Gro. BH25 48 E3
Queens Pk Av. BH8 30 D6
Queens Pk Gdns. BH8 41 F1
Queens Park Rd. BH8 41 F1
Queens Park Sth Dri.
BH8 41 F1
Queens Park West Dri.
BH8 31 E6
Queens Rd. BH2 39 G4
Queens Rd. BH23 44 D4
Queens Rd. BH21 19 C6
Queens Rd. BH22 17 E1
Queens Rd. BH14 38 B3
Queens Way. BH24 8 D5
Queensland Rd. BH5 42 A4
Queensway. BH25 47 H2
Queenswood Av. BH23 31 G5
Queenswood Dri. BH22 17 E2
Quince La. BH21 14 D3
Quintin Clo. BH23 46 C4
Quomp. BH24 8 C5

R.L. Stevenson Av. BH4 39 F4
Radipole Rd. BH17 27 F2
Raglan Gdns. BH11 29 E2
Raleigh Clo. BH23 45 F5
Raleigh Rd. SO41 48 B4
Raleigh Rd. BH12 28 C3
Ralph Rd. BH21 18 D4
Randolph Rd. BH1 41 G4
Randolph Rd. BH14 37 H2
Ranelagh Rd. BH23 46 C5
Raven Way. BH23 45 F5
Ravens Way. SO41 51 E5
Ravenscourt Rd. BH6 42 C4
Ravensdale Clo. BH12 38 A1
Ravine Rd. BH5 42 B5
Ravine Rd. BH13 53 F1
Rayleigh Clo. BH24 9 E4
Raymond Clo. BH31 6 E2
Rayners Dri. BH12 38 C2
Rebbeck Rd. BH7 42 A3
Recreation Rd. BH12 38 B1
Rectory Av. BH21 18 C3
Rectory Rd. BH15 36 B1
Red La. BH21 18 A3
Red Oaks Clo. BH22 16 D2
Redan Clo. BH23 46 D5
Redbreast Rd. BH9 30 C3
Redbreast Rd Nth. BH9 30 C2
Redcliffe Clo. BH23 33 G4
Redcotts La. BH21 14 B4
Redcotts Rd. BH21 14 A4
Redhill Av. BH9 30 A4
Redhill Clo. BH9 30 A3
Redhill Cres. BH9 30 B3
Redhill Dri. BH9 30 A4
Redhoave Rd. BH17 27 E3
Redhorn Clo. BH16 35 C5
Redlands. BH12 38 D2
Redmans Vw. BH31 6 B2
Redshank Clo. BH17 34 F1
Redvers Rd. BH23 44 D3
Redwood Clo. BH24 8 D5
Redwood Dri. BH22 10 C6
Redwood Rd. BH16 34 A2
Regency Cres. BH23 33 E6
Regency Pl. BH24 8 C4
Regent Dri. BH7 31 H6
Regent Way. BH23 43 H3
Reid St. BH23 43 G1
Rempstone Rd. BH21 20 C2
Renault Dri. BH18 26 A3
*Restynge Ho,
Ringwood Rd. BH31 6 C1
Retreat Rd. BH21 14 C4
Reuben Dri. BH15 35 D7
Rhiners Clo. SO41 54 B3
Ribble Clo. BH18 26 A2
Ricardo Cres. BH23 45 G4
Rice Gdns. BH16 35 D5
Richard Clo. BH16 34 B2
Richie Pl. BH22 11 E2
Richmond Bri Rd. BH8 41 F2
Richmond Gdns. BH1 5 D1
Richmond Hill. BH2 5 C2

Richmond Hill Dri. BH2 5 C1
Richmond Pk Av. BH8 40 D1
*Richmond Pk Clo,
Holdenhurst. BH8 41 F2
Richmond Pk Cres. BH8 41 E1
Richmond Pk Rd. BH8 40 D1
Richmond Rd. BH14 38 B2
Richmond Rd. BH21 14 C5
Richmond Wood Rd.
BH8 40 D1
Ridge Way. BH22 23 G2
Ridgefield Gdns. BH23 46 B4
Ridgemount Gdns.
BH15 35 E6
Ridgeway. BH18 26 B1
Ridgeway. BH21 18 C3
Ridley Rd. BH9 30 B5
Ridout Clo. BH10 29 F4
Riggs Gdns. BH11 28 D3
Rigler Rd. BH15 36 A6
Rimbury Way. BH23 33 E6
Ringwood Rd,
Bransgore. BH23 54 B1
Ringwood Rd. BH22 17 E5
Ringwood Rd,
Hinton. BH23 46 B1
Ringwood Rd. BH14 37 E3
Ringwood Rd. BH24 12 A6
Ringwood Rd. BH21 7 B7
Ringwood Rd. BH31 6 C1
Ringwood Rd. BH11 22 B6
Ringwood Rd. BH22 11 G6
Ringwood-Bournemouth
Spur Rd. BH24 13 G6
Ringwood-by-Pass.
BH24 8 A6
Ripon Rd. BH9 30 C5
Ritchie Rd. BH11 29 E1
River Clo. BH21 14 B3
River Gdns. SO41 51 E5
River Way. BH23 32 C5
Riverdale La. BH23 43 G2
Riverlea Rd. BH23 43 G3
Rivermead Gdns. BH23 32 C4
Riverside. BH24 8 B5
Riverside Av. BH8 32 A4
Riverside La. BH6 43 F4
Riverside Rd. BH6 43 F4
Riverside Rd. BH22 10 D4
*Riverslea Mews,
Russell Dri. BH23 44 D4
Roberts Clo. SO41 55 C3
Roberts La. BH17 34 F2
Roberts Rd. BH17 26 B3
Roberts Rd. BH7 42 A3
Robins Clo. BH18 20 A3
Robin Gro. BH25 49 B5
Robins Way. BH23 45 G5
Robinswood Dri. BH22 17 F1
Robsall Clo. BH12 28 C6
Rochester Rd. BH11 29 E1
Rockbourne Gdns.
BH25 47 G5
Rockford Clo. BH6 43 F5
Rockley Rd. BH15 35 E7
Rodbourne Clo. SO41 55 B4
Rodney Clo. BH12 29 E5
Rodney Dri. BH23 45 F4
Rodway. BH21 14 C5
Rodwell Clo. BH10 23 F5
Roebuck Clo. BH25 48 D4
Roeshot Cres. BH23 46 B4
Roeshot Hill. BH23 45 H1
Rolls Dri. BH6 43 H5
Roman Heights. BH21 18 D4
Roman Rd. BH18 19 D8
Romney Clo. BH10 30 A2
Romney Rd. BH10 30 A2
Rook Hill Rd. BH23 45 H4
Rookcliff Way. SO41 50 D5
Roosevelt Cres. BH11 23 E4
Ropers La. BH16 34 D3
Ropley Rd. BH7 42 C2
Rosamund Av. BH11 20 D2
Roscrea Clo. BH6 43 H4
Roscrea Dri. BH6 43 H4
Rose Cres. BH15 27 F6
Rose Gdns. BH9 30 B3
Roseberry Clo. BH31 6 F3
Rosebery Rd. BH5 42 B4
Rosebud Av. BH9 30 B3
Rosecrae Clo. BH25 48 B3
Rosedale Clo. BH23 45 E4
Rosehill Clo. BH23 54 B1
Rosehill Dri. BH23 54 B1

Rosemary Gdns. BH12 27 H5
Rosemary Rd. BH12 27 H5
Rosemount Rd. BH4 39 F5
Rosewood Gdns. BH25 48 B3
Roslin Rd. BH3 30 A6
Roslin Rd South. BH3 40 A1
Ross Gdns. BH11 22 A5
Ross Rd. BH24 9 F2
Rossglades. BH3 40 B2
Rossley Rd. BH23 46 B3
Rosslin Rd. BH3 29 H5
Rossmore Rd. BH12 27 H4
Rotary Clo. BH21 15 E2
Rothbury Pk. BH25 49 D5
Rotherfield Rd. BH5 42 B5
Rotherfield Rd. BH23 46 D4
Rothesay Dri. BH23 46 B5
Rothesay Rd. BH4 39 G1
Rotterdam Dri. BH23 44 C3
Roumelia La. BH5 41 H4
Roundhaye Rd. BH11 22 C5
Roundways. BH11 28 D2
Rowan Clo. BH23 46 B4
Rowan Clo. BH24 12 B4
Rowan Clo. SO41 54 B4
Rowan Dri. BH23 46 A4
Rowan Dri. BH17 34 E1
Rowan Dri. BH31 6 E3
Rowbarrow Clo. BH17 27 E2
Rowena Rd. BH6 43 F4
Rowland Av. BH15 36 D1
Rowlands Hill. BH21 14 C4
Rownham Rd. BH8 31 E2
Royal Arcade. BH1 41 G4
Royal Oak Rd. BH10 23 E5
Royster Clo. BH17 26 C4
Royston Pl. BH25 49 D7
Rozelle Rd. BH14 37 H3
Rubens Clo. BH23 48 C3
Rufford Gdns. BH6 43 E4
Rugby Rd. BH17 26 A3
Runnymede Av. BH11 22 A4
Runton Rd. BH12 38 D2
Rushall La. BH21 19 A6
Rushcombe Way. BH21 19 D5
Rushford Warren. BH23 45 H5
Rushmere Rd. BH6 42 D2
Rushton Cres. BH3 40 C2
Ruskin Av. BH9 30 C2
Russel Rd. BH10 23 F4
Russell Cotes Rd. BH1 5 E3
Russell Dri. BH23 44 D4
Russell Gdns. BH16 35 C6
Russell Gdns. BH23 13 F2
Russet Clo. BH22 17 E2
Rutland Rd. BH9 30 C5
Rutland Rd. BH23 33 E5
Ryall Rd. BH17 26 D3
Ryan Clo. BH22 17 E1
Ryan Gdns. BH22 17 E2
Rydal Clo. BH23 32 C2
Ryecroft Av. BH11 22 B5

St Georges Dri. BH22 17 E5
St Helier Rd. BH12 28 B3
St Ives End La. BH24 13 E3
St Ives Gdns. BH2 40 C3
St Ives Park. BH24 13 F2
St Ives Wood. BH24 13 F2
St James Rd. BH22 16 C3
St James Sq. BH5 42 A4
St James's Clo. BH16 36 B6
St James Rd. SO41 54 C3
St Johns Clo. BH21 14 C5
St Johns Gdns. BH9 30 B4
St Johns Hill. BH21 14 C4
St Johns Mews. BH9 30 B3
St Johns Rd. BH5 41 G4
St Johns Rd. BH23 13 F2
St Johns Rd. BH15 36 D3
St Just Clo. BH17 26 D6
St Ledgers Pl. BH8 41 F2
St Ledgers Rd. BH8 41 F1
St Leonards Rd. BH8 40 D2
St Leonards Way. BH24 12 B2
St Lukes Rd. BH3 40 B1
St Margarets Av. BH23 44 B4
St Margarets Clo. BH23 14 A3
St Margarets Hill. BH21 14 A3
St Margarets Rd. BH10 29 F3
St Margarets Rd. BH15 36 D3
St Marks Rd. BH11 29 F2
St Martins Rd. BH16 34 A3
St Marys Clo. BH23 54 C1
St Marys Gro. SO41 55 C2
St Marys Rd. BH1 41 G4
St Marys Rd. BH22 17 E4
St Marys Rd. BH15 36 D4
St Merrins Clo. BH10 29 G1
St Michaels Clo. BH31 6 C3
St Michaels Clo. BH15 35 E7
St Michaels Rd. BH2 5 B7
St Michaels Rd. BH31 6 C3
St Osmunds Rd. BH14 38 B3
St Pauls La. BH8 40 D4
St Pauls Pl. BH8 40 D4
St Pauls Rd. BH8 40 D4
St Peters Clo. BH1 5 D2
St Peters Rd. BH14 37 G3
St Saviours Clo. BH7 42 C1
St Stephens La. BH31 6 D1
St Stephens Rd. BH2 5 B1
St Stephens Way. BH2 5 C1
St Swithuns Rd. BH1 40 D4
St Thomas Clo. BH10 29 H2
St Valerie Rd. BH2 40 B3
St Winifreds Rd. BH2 40 B3
Saints Clo. BH21 7 B7
Salerno Pl. BH15 35 D7
Salisbury Rd. BH1 41 G4
Salisbury Rd. BH14 37 H2
Salisbury Rd. BH24 8 C4
Salisbury Rd. BH23 33 G1
Salter Rd. BH13 52 C6
Salterns Rd. BH14 37 G4
Salterns Way. BH14 52 B1
Saltgrass La. SO41 51 G6
Saltings La. BH16 34 B3
Samples Way. BH17 27 F5
Samson Rd. BH15 35 D6
Sancreed Rd. BH12 28 C6
Sandbanks Rd. BH14 37 E4
Sandbourne Rd. BH4 39 F6
Sandbourne Rd. BH15 36 D3
Sandcotes Rd. BH14 37 H3
Sanderlings. BH24 9 E2
Sandford Clo. BH9 31 E2
Sandford Way. BH18 19 F8
Sandhills Clo. BH17 26 D3
Sandhurst Dri. BH21 7 D8
Sandmartin Clo. BH25 49 B8
Sandown Rd. BH23 45 E4
Sandpiper Clo. BH17 34 F1
Sandpit La. BH15 36 D4
Sandringham Clo. BH9 30 D1
Sandringham Gdns.
BH9 30 D1
Sandringham Rd.
BH14 37 H1
Sandy Clo. BH21 15 F1
Sandy La. BH23 32 D4
Sandy La. BH24 12 D3
Sandy La. BH6 42 C3
Sandy La. BH16 34 A3
Sandy La. BH21 7 B6
Sandy La. BH31 6 D2
Sandy La. BH21 15 F1
Sandy Mead Rd. BH8 31 G5
Sandy Plot. BH23 33 H6

Sandy Way. BH10 30 A2
Sandyhurst Clo. BH17 26 C4
Sarah Clo. BH7 31 H6
Sarah Sands Clo. BH23 44 D2
Sark Rd. BH12 28 B5
Sarum Avenue Nth.
BH22 11 E2
Sarum Avenue Sth.
BH22 11 E2
Sarum St. BH15 36 B6
Saulfland Dri. BH23 46 A4
Saulfland Pl. BH23 46 A4
Saxon Sq. BH23 43 H2
Saxon King Gdns. BH6 43 G5
Saxonbury Rd. BH6 43 E3
Saxonford Rd. BH23 45 H3
Saxonhurst Clo. BH10 30 A1
Saxonhurst Gdns.
BH10 23 G6
Saxonhurst Rd. BH10 30 A2
Scarf Rd. BH17 27 F5
School La, Milford-
on-Sea. SO41 51 E3
School La. BH11 23 E5
School La,
Ringwood. BH24 8 C5
School La,
St Ives. BH24 13 E3
School La. BH15 36 C2
School La, Three Legged
Cross. BH21 7 D8
School La, Wimborne
Minster. BH21 14 B3
Scott Clo. BH12 28 D4
Scott Rd. BH12 28 D4
Scotter Rd. BH7 42 B3
Scotts Grn. BH23 45 F2
Scotts Hill La. BH23 44 C3
Sea Rd. BH25 49 A6
Sea Rd. BH5 41 G5
Sea Rd. SO41 51 E5
Sea Rd. BH6 47 G5
Sea View Rd. BH25 47 G5
Sea View Rd. BH12 37 G2
Sea View Rd. BH16 34 A3
Sea Vixen Ind Est.
BH23 45 F3
Seaview Rd. BH23 47 F3
Sea Winds. SO41 50 B4
Seabank Clo. BH16 34 A3
Seabourne Pl. BH5 42 B4
Seabourne Rd. BH5 42 B3
Seacombe Rd. BH13 52 B6
Seacroft Av. BH25 49 A7
Seafield Clo. BH25 49 B7
Seafield Dri. BH6 43 E3
Seafield Rd. BH25 49 A7
Seafield Rd. BH23 45 H4
Seafield Rd. BH6 43 E4
Seagull Rd. BH8 31 F4
Seamoor La. BH4 39 F4
Seamoor Rd. BH4 39 F4
Seaton Clo. BH23 47 E4
Seaton Rd. BH23 47 E4
Seatown Clo. BH17 27 G3
Seaward Av. BH25 49 A7
Seaward Av. BH6 42 C5
Seaway. BH25 49 D6
Seaway Av. BH23 45 H3
Second Marine Av.
BH25 49 C8
Sedgley Rd. BH9 30 A6
Selby Clo. BH18 26 A1
Seldown. BH15 36 D4
Seldown Bridge. BH15 36 D5
Seldown La. BH15 36 C4
Seldown Rd. BH15 36 D4
Selfridge Av. BH6 43 H5
Selfridge Clo. BH6 43 H5
Seliot Clo. BH15 36 D2
Selkirk Clo. BH21 21 E2
Sellwood Way. BH25 47 G4
Selworthy Clo. BH14 37 G5
Serpentine La Sth.
BH15 36 C4
Serpentine Rd. BH15 36 C4
Set Thorns Rd. SO41 54 C3
Setley Gdns. BH8 31 F3
Sevenoaks Dri. BH7 42 B1
Severn Rd. BH22 17 H5
Seymour Rd. BH24 8 D3
Shackleton Sq. BH23 54 C1
Shaftesbury Clo. BH22 11 F4
Shaftesbury Rd. BH8 41 E2
Shaftesbury Rd. BH15 36 D4
Shaftesbury Rd. BH22 11 F4

Shakespeare Rd. BH21 14 B3
Shakespeare Rd. BH6 42 D2
Shapland Av. BH11 22 B6
Shapwick Rd. BH15 36 A6
Shard Clo. BH31 6 D2
Sharlands Clo. BH18 26 B1
Sharp Rd. BH12 29 E6
Sharvells Rd. SO41 50 C4
Shaves La. BH25 48 C2
Shaw Rd. BH24 9 F2
Shawford Gdns. BH8 31 F3
Shawford Rd. BH8 31 F3
Shearbrook Clo. BH23 54 C1
Shelbourne Rd. BH8 40 D2
Sheldrake Gdns. SO41 55 C1
Sheldrake Rd. BH23 45 F5
Shelley Clo. BH24 12 C2
Shelley Clo. BH1 41 G3
Shelley Clo. BH23 46 A5
Shelley Gdns. BH1 41 G3
Shelley Hill. BH23 46 A5
Shelley Rd. BH1 41 G3
Shelley Rd. BH12 38 B2
Shelley Way. SO41 51 E4
Shelton Rd. BH6 42 C3
Shepherd Clo. BH23 46 C3
Shepherds Field. BH21 14 B3
Shepherds Way. BH7 42 B1
Sherborn Cres. BH7 27 F3
Sherborne Dri. BH22 17 F5
Sherfield Clo. BH8 31 E3
Sheringham Rd. BH12 38 D2
Sherrin Clo. BH15 36 D2
Sherwood Av. BH22 17 E5
Sherwood Clo. BH23 43 F1
Sherwood Dri. BH31 6 E1
Shillingstone Dri. BH9 30 D2
*Shillington Gdns,
  Melbury Av. BH12 28 D5
Shillito Rd. BH12 38 C2
Shinglebank Dri. SO41 50 D5
Shipstal Clo. BH16 35 C5
Shires Mead. BH31 6 D2
Shirley Clo. BH23 54 C1
Shirley Clo. BH22 11 F4
Shirley Rd. BH9 30 C5
Shirley Rd. BH12 37 H1
Shirley Rd. BH16 34 B2
Shore Av. BH16 34 B4
Shore Clo. SO41 51 E5
Shore Clo. BH16 34 C4
Shore Gdns. BH16 34 B4
Shore La. BH16 34 B4
Shore Rd. BH13 52 D2
Shorefield Cres. SO41 50 D3
Shorefield Rd. SO41 50 C2
Shorefield Way. SO41 50 D3
Short Clo. BH12 29 E4
Shorts Clo. BH23 33 H5
Shottsford Rd. BH15 36 C2
Sidney Gdns. BH9 30 D1
Silchester Clo. BH2 40 B3
Silver Birch Clo. BH4 39 E3
Silver Business Pk.
  BH23 45 E3
Silver St. BH23 44 B4
Silver St. SO41 55 B1
Silver Way. BH23 46 C5
Silverdale. BH25 49 D7
Silverdale Clo. BH18 19 E7
Silverwood Clo. BH21 20 C1
Simmonds Clo. BH12 36 D2
Singleton Dri. BH10 29 G3
Siskin Clo. BH22 16 D1
Sixpenny Clo. BH12 28 D5
Skinner St. BH15 36 C6
Skipton Clo. BH18 26 A3
Sky End La. SO41 55 C2
Slade Clo. SO41 55 C1
Slades Farm Rd. BH10 29 G3
Slades La. BH10 29 G3
Sleepbrook Clo. BH31 6 B2
Sleight La. BH21 18 C3
Slepe Cres. BH12 28 D5
Slinn Rd. BH23 44 D3
Slip Way. BH15 36 B5
Slough La. BH16 34 A3
Smithfield Pl. BH9 30 B5
Smithson Clo. BH12 29 F5
Smithy La. BH25 48 B1
Smugglers La. BH21 14 D1
Smugglers La Nth.
  BH23 46 A4
Smugglers La Sth.
  BH23 46 B4

Smugglers Wood Rd.
  BH23 46 A4
Snails La. BH24 8 C1
Snowdon Rd. BH4 39 F3
Snowdrop Gdns. BH23 45 H1
Soberton Rd. BH8 41 F1
Solent Dri. BH25 49 C7
Solent Pines. SO41 50 C4
Solent Prom. BH6 43 F6
Solent Rd. BH25 47 G5
Solent Rd. BH6 43 G6
Solent Rd. BH23 47 E3
Solent Way. SO41 51 F4
Solly Clo. BH12 28 C5
Soloman Way. BH15 35 D7
Somerby Rd. BH15 36 D1
Somerford Av. BH23 45 G2
Somerford Business Pk.
  BH23 45 F3
Somerford Rd. BH23 45 E3
Somerford Way. BH23 45 E3
Somerley Rd. BH9 30 C6
Somerley Vw. BH24 9 F2
Somerset Rd. BH23 43 E1
Somerset Rd. BH7 42 A3
Somerton Clo. BH25 48 F4
Somerville Rd. BH21 5 A3
Somerville Rd. BH24 9 F2
Sonning Way. BH8 30 D4
Sopers La. BH23 43 G3
Sopers La. BH17 26 A4
Sopley Clo. BH25 47 G5
Sopwith Clo. BH23 45 G4
Sopwith Cres. BH21 20 D1
Sorrel Gdns. BH18 Inset 19
Sorrel Ct. BH23 45 G2
Sorrell Way. BH23 45 G2
South Av. BH25 49 D5
South Cliff Rd. BH2 5 D3
South Field. BH24 8 C6
South Haven Clo. BH16 35 B6
South Kinson Dri.
  BH11 22 D6
South Park Rd. BH12 29 E5
South Rd, Boscombe.
  BH1 41 G3
South Rd, Bournemouth.
  BH1 40 C6
South Rd. BH21 19 D5
South Rd. BH15 36 C5
South Sway La. SO41 54 C4
South View Pl. BH2 5 D3
South View Rd. BH23 43 G3
South Western Cres.
  BH14 37 G5
Southampton Rd. BH24 8 C4
Southbourne Coast Rd.
  BH6 43 E6
Southbourne Gro. BH6 42 C4
Southbourne
  Overcliff Dri. BH6 42 C5
Southbourne
  Promenade. BH6 42 C6
Southbourne Rd. BH6 42 B3
Southbrook Clo. BH17 27 G3
Southcliffe Rd. BH25 47 G5
Southcliffe Rd. BH23 45 H4
Southcote Rd. BH1 41 F4
Southdown Way. BH22 11 F5
Southern Av. BH22 11 G5
Southern La. BH25 49 B6
Southern Oaks. BH25 49 B6
Southern Rd. BH6 42 C5
Southernhay Rd. BH31 6 E2
Southey Rd. BH23 45 E2
Southfield Mews. BH24 8 C6
Southill Av. BH12 28 B6
Southill Gdns. BH9 30 C5
Southill Rd. BH12 38 B1
Southill Rd. BH9 30 C5
Southill Rd,
  Rossmore. BH12 28 B6
Southlands Av. BH21 19 D5
Southlands Av. BH6 43 F4
Southlands Clo. BH21 19 D5
Southlawns Wk. BH25 49 B6
Southlea Av. BH6 43 F4
Southville Rd. BH9 30 B5
Southwood Av. BH23 47 E3
Southwood Av. BH6 42 D2
Southwood Clo. BH22 17 E3
Southwood Clo. BH23 47 E3
Sovereign Business Pk.
  BH15 36 B1

Sovereign Centre. BH1 41 G4
Sovereign Clo. BH7 31 H6
Sparkford Clo. BH7 42 B1
Speedwell Dri. BH23 45 G2
Spencer Rd. BH1 41 E4
Spencer Rd. BH13 53 E1
Spencer Rd. BH25 48 C4
Spetisbury Clo. BH9 30 D2
Spicer La. BH11 22 B6
Spinacre. BH25 49 D7
Spindle Clo. BH18 Inset 19
Spindlewood Clo. BH25 49 C6
Spinners Clo. BH22 11 E5
Spinney Clo. BH24 12 B3
Spinney Way. BH25 48 C1
Spinneys La. BH22 17 E4
Spittlefields. BH24 9 E5
Spring Clo. BH31 6 C3
Spring Gdns. BH12 38 B2
Spring La. BH25 48 F4
Spring Rd. BH1 41 E3
Springbank Rd. BH7 42 A1
Springdale Av. BH18 19 F6
Springdale Gro. BH21 19 D7
Springdale Rd. BH18 19 C7
Springfield Av. BH23 32 C4
Springfield Av. BH6 43 F4
Springfield Clo. BH31 6 C3
Springfield Cres. BH14 37 G3
Springfield Gdns. BH25 48 F4
Springfield Rd. BH14 37 G2
Springfield Rd. BH31 6 C3
Springvale Av. BH7 42 A1
Springwater Clo. BH11 29 E1
Springwater Rd. BH11 29 E1
Spruce Clo. BH17 34 E1
Spur Clo. BH21 15 D3
Spur Hill Av. BH14 38 B4
Spur Rd. BH14 38 B3
Spurgeon Rd. BH7 42 B3
Square Clo. BH21 16 B5
Squirrel Walk. BH31 6 C3
Squirrels Clo. BH23 32 C4
Stacey Clo. BH12 28 B6
Stacey Gdns. BH8 31 G3
Stafford Rd. BH1 5 F1
Stag Clo. BH25 48 A3
Stagswood. BH31 6 A2
Stalbridge Dri. BH22 17 E5
Stalbridge Rd. BH17 26 B5
Stalham Rd. BH12 38 D1
Stallards La. BH24 8 B4
Stamford Rd. BH6 42 D2
Stanfield Clo. BH12 28 B5
Stanfield Rd. BH22 16 D2
Stanfield Rd. BH12 28 B5
Stanfield Rd. BH9 30 A6
Stanford Rise. SO41 54 B3
*Staniforth Ct,
  Stony La Sth. BH23 44 C4
Stanley Clo. BH31 6 D2
Stanley Green Cres.
  BH15 36 B2
Stanley Green Rd.
  BH15 36 B2
Stanley Rd. BH1 41 E3
Stanley Rd. BH23 46 D5
Stanley Rd. BH15 36 C6
Stannington Clo. BH25 49 C5
Stanpit. BH23 44 D4
Stanton Rd. BH10 29 G2
Staple Close La. BH15 36 C1
Staplecross La. BH24 42 D2
Stapleford Av. BH22 17 G2
Stapehill Cres. BH21 16 H4
Stapehill Rd. BH21 16 B6
Star La. BH24 8 B5
Station App. BH23 43 G2
Station Rd. BH23 46 C2
Station Rd. BH25 48 C4
Station Rd. BH14 37 G3
Station Rd. BH15 36 A6
Station Rd. BH31 6 A1
Station Rd. BH22 11 E2
Station Rd. SO41 54 B3
Station Ter. BH21 14 C5
Stedman Rd. BH6 42 C4
Steeple Clo. BH17 26 C1
Steepleton Rd. BH18 26 C2
Stem La. BH25 48 A2
Stenhurst Rd. BH15 36 D1
Stephen Langton Dri.
  BH11 22 A6
Sterte Av. BH15 36 B3

Sterte Av West. BH15 36 B3
Sterte Clo. BH15 36 B3
Sterte Esplanade.
  BH15 36 C4
Sterte Ind Est. BH15 36 C4
Sterte Rd. BH15 36 C3
Stevenson Clo. BH21 14 C5
Stevenson Cres. BH14 38 C4
Stevenson Rd. BH6 43 G6
Stewart Clo. BH8 41 E3
Stewart Rd. BH8 40 D2
Stewarts Way. BH22 17 G1
Stillmore Rd. BH11 28 C1
Stinsford Clo. BH9 30 D1
Stinsford Rd. BH17 26 D4
Stirling Clo. BH25 48 D4
Stirling Rd. BH3 30 A6
Stirling Way. BH23 45 G4
Stirrup Clo. BH21 15 H2
Stirrup Clo. BH16 34 D2
Stoborough Dri. BH18 26 A2
Stockbridge Dri. BH17 27 G2
Stoke Wood Rd. BH3 40 B2
Stokes Av. BH15 36 C3
Stone Gdns. BH8 31 H3
Stone La. BH21 14 A3
Stonechat Clo. BH22 10 C6
Stonecrop Clo. BH18 Inset 19
Stoneleigh Av. SO41 55 B1
Stony La. BH23 33 G3
Stony La Sth. BH23 44 C4
Stopples La. SO41 55 B1
Stora La. BH18 26 B1
Stour Rd. BH8 41 F2
Stour Rd. BH23 43 G2
Stour Walk. BH8 31 F1
Stour Way. BH23 32 C5
Stourbank Rd. BH23 43 G3
Stourcliffe Av. BH6 42 C5
Stourcroft Dri. BH23 32 C4
Stourfield Rd. BH5 42 B4
Stourpaine Rd. BH17 26 D2
Stourvale Av. BH23 32 C6
Stourvale Pl. BH5 42 B3
Stourvale Rd. BH6 42 B3
Stourview Gdns. BH21 18 E2
Stourwood Av. BH6 42 D5
Stourwood Rd. BH6 42 D5
Stouts La. BH23 54 B1
Strand St. BH15 36 B6
Stratfield Pl. BH25 47 H2
Strathmore Dri. BH31 6 E1
Strathmore Rd. BH9 30 B1
Stratton Rd. BH9 31 E2
Strete Mt. BH23 45 E3
Stretton Ct. BH14 37 G3
Strides La. BH24 8 B5
Strode Gdns. BH24 13 F2
Stroud Clo. BH21 15 F2
Stroud Gdns. BH23 45 E4
Stroud La. BH23 45 E4
Stroud Park Av. BH23 45 E3
Strouden Av. BH8 30 D5
Strouden Rd. BH9 30 B5
Struan Clo. BH24 12 D1
Struan Ct. BH24 13 E1
Struan Dri. BH24 12 D1
Struan Gdns. BH24 12 D1
Stuart Clo. BH16 34 B2
Stuart Rd. BH23 47 E5
Studland Rd. BH4 39 F6
Studlands Dri. SO41 50 C4
Studley Clo. BH23 47 F4
Studley Clo. BH25 47 G5
Sturminster Rd. BH9 30 D1
Suffolk Av. BH23 33 E5
Suffolk Clo. BH21 15 H2
Suffolk Rd. BH2 5 B2
Suffolk Rd Sth. BH2 39 H3
Summercroft Way.
  BH22 11 F3
Summerfield Clo.
  BH23 33 G4
Summerfield Clo.
  BH21 15 G6
Summerfields. BH7 31 G6
Summerfields. BH31 6 C3
Summers Av. BH11 22 D5
Summers La. BH23 44 D1
Summertrees Ct. BH25 48 F3
Sunbury Clo. BH11 22 C5
Sunderland Dri. BH23 45 H3
Sundew Clo. BH25 48 F3
Sundew Rd. BH23 45 H1
Sundew Rd. BH18 Inset 19

Sunningdale Cres.
  BH10 29 G1
Sunny Hill Rd. BH12 38 B2
Sunnybank Dri. BH21 15 G3
Sunnybank Rd. BH21 15 G3
Sunnybank Way. BH21 15 G3
Sunnyfield Rd. BH25 49 C7
Sunnyhill Rd. BH6 42 C4
Sunnylands Av. BH6 43 F4
Sunnymoor Rd. BH11 29 E4
Sunnyside Rd. BH12 38 B1
Sunridge Clo. BH12 39 E1
Surrey Clo. BH23 33 E4
Surrey Gdns. BH4 39 G3
Surrey Rd. BH4 39 H3
Surrey Rd South. BH4 39 G3
Sussex Clo. BH9 30 D1
Sutherland Av. BH18 19 E6
Sutton Clo. BH17 27 G2
Sutton Rd. BH9 30 C5
Swallow Clo. BH17 34 F2
Swallow Dri. SO41 51 F5
Swallow Way. BH21 15 F1
Swan Mead. BH24 9 F6
Swanmore Clo. BH7 42 C2
Swanmore Rd. BH7 42 B2
Swan Mead. BH24 9 E6
Swansbury Dri. BH8 32 A4
Sway Gdns. BH8 31 F3
Sway Rd. BH25 48 C1
Swift Clo. BH17 34 F2
Swordfish Dri. BH23 45 G3
Sycamore Clo. BH23 32 C6
Sycamore Clo. SO41 50 D4
Sycamore Clo. BH17 34 F1
*Sycamore Ct,
  Linbrook Dri. BH24 9 E2
Sycamore Rd. SO41 55 B1
Sydling Clo. BH17 27 G2
Sydney Rd. BH18 26 A2
Sydney Rd. BH23 32 D5
Sylmor Gdns. BH9 30 C4
Sylvan Clo. SO41 55 D2
Sylvan Clo. BH24 12 B3
Sylvan Rd. BH12 37 H1
Symes Rd. BH15 35 D5

Tadden Walk. BH18 19 F8
Tait Clo. BH17 27 E5
Talbot Av. BH3 30 A6
Talbot Clo. BH3 46 C3
Talbot Dri. BH12 29 E5
Talbot Hill Rd. BH9 29 H5
Talbot Meadows. BH12 29 F4
Talbot Mews. BH10 29 E4
Talbot Rise. BH10 29 G3
Talbot Rd. BH9 30 A6
Tamar Clo. BH24 17 H5
Tamworth Rd. BH7 42 A3
Tan Howse Clo. BH7 32 A6
Tanglewood Ct. BH25 48 C4
Tangmere Clo. BH23 45 G4
Tapper Ct, BH21 14 D5
Tarn Dri. BH17 26 A4
Tarrant Rd. BH17 27 E1
Tarrant Rd. BH9 30 D2
Tasman Clo. BH23 33 E6
Tatnam La. BH15 36 C3
Tatnam Rd. BH15 36 C3
Taverner Clo. BH15 36 D5
Taylor Rd. BH8 31 E2
Teasel Way. BH22 11 F5
Tedder Clo. BH11 29 F1
Tedder Gdns. BH11 29 F1
Tedder Rd. BH11 29 F1
Telford Rd. BH21 16 B1
Templer Clo. BH11 28 D3
Tennyson Rd. BH9 30 B3
Tennyson Rd. BH14 37 G4
Tennyson Rd. BH21 14 B3
Tensing Rd. BH23 44 D2
Terence Av. BH17 26 C3
Terence Rd. BH21 19 C6
Tern Ct. BH6 42 D3
Terrace Mount. BH2 5 B2
Terrace Rd. BH2 5 B2
Terrington Av. BH23 46 B3
Thames Alley. BH16 36 B6
Thames St. BH15 36 B6
The Acorns. BH1 15 G4
The Arcade. BH1 5 D2
The Avenue. BH9 31 B3
The Avenue. BH22 11 E3
The Avenue. BH13 53 G1
The Beeches. BH7 42 A1